EDITOR: LEE JOHNSON

OSPREY MILITARY **WARRIOR SERIES** 14

ZULU
1816–1906

Text by
IAN KNIGHT
Colour plates by
ANGUS McBRIDE

First published in Great Britain in 1995 by
Osprey, an imprint of Reed Consumer Books Ltd.
Michelin House, 81 Fulham Road,
London SW3 6RB
and Auckland, Melbourne, Singapore and Toronto

ISBN 1 85532 474 1

Filmset in Great Britain
Printed through World Print Ltd, Hong Kong

Publisher's note
Readers may wish to study this title in conjunction with
the following Osprey publications:
MAA 198 *British Army on Campaign (3) 1856–81*
MAA 212 *Victoria's Enemies (1) Southern Africa*
Campaign 14 *The Zulu War 1879*
Elite 21 *The Zulus*
Elite 32 *British Forces in Zululand 1879*

Artist's note
Readers may care to note that the original paintings
from which the colour plates in this book were pre-
pared are available for private sale. All reproduction
copyright whatsoever is retained by the publisher. All
enquiries should be addressed to:
Scorpio Gallery
PO Box 475
Hailsham
E. Sussex BN27 2SL
The publishers regret that they can enter into no
correspondence upon this matter.

ZULU 1816–1906

HISTORICAL BACKGROUND

The Zulu kingdom in its independent form existed for a surprisingly short time. It emerged during a period of conquest in the 1820s, and was broken by the British in the Anglo-Zulu war of 1879. However, in the same way that the line of the Zulu Royal House has continued, unbroken, into modern times so the ethos of the old Zulu military system continued to dominate the thought-patterns of the Zulu-speaking peoples long after the Zulu army itself had been dispersed. Indeed, the repercussions of the rise and fall of the old Zulu kingdom continue to influence events in the post-apartheid Republic of South Africa today.

It is one of the many ironies of this saga that the successes of the Zulu kingdom have led to the name Zulu being applied indiscriminately to the language and culture of many broadly similar African groups, only some of which ever acknowledged their allegiance to the Zulu kings. The Zulus were originally just one of a number of extended social units – called for convenience' sake 'clans' – who inhabited the northern sector of the eastern sea-board of southern Africa, from the Umzimvubu river in the south to the Phongolo in the north, in the late 18th century. All of them spoke the same language, allowing for differences in regional dialects, and possessed a culture based on polygamy and cattle. The people lived in largely self-contained homesteads, and owed political allegiance to a hereditary chieftain. About the turn of the century, however, the Zulu society collapsed into violence, and a new, more sophisticated political order emerged. In its most developed form, this new order found expression in the Zulu kingdom.

Influence of King Shaka

The reason for the change is a matter of debate. Certainly the late 18th century was a time of drought and famine, and it is possible that chiefdoms banded together or conquered their neighbours in an attempt to control a wider range of natural resources. Equally, the change may have corresponded with an intensive trading drive by the Portuguese enclave at Mozambique, which upset the neighbouring African economic status quo and led to chiefs attempting to dominate lucrative trade routes. For whatever reason, it was out of this violence that the Zulu

Daily life: a group of Zulus outside a typical hut, photographed some time in the 19th century. As this picture suggests, it was the lot of unmarried girls to carry food for their fathers and brothers.

An insizwa *or unmarried man in the 19th century. Fashionable young men worked their hair up into* fantastic shapes such as this, with tallow and clay. (Killie Campbell Africana Library)

Mfolozi river in the north and the Thukela in the south, although significant areas outside this region either acknowledged King Shaka's authority or were depopulated as the groups who inhabited them retired out of his reach.

Administration

The Zulu kingdom was by no means politically monolithic. It remained a conglomerate of clans; some of these had been defeated by Shaka and incorporated by force, but others had joined as allies, and retained a good deal of local autonomy. The latter retained their chiefly lines, which in turn provided a level of regional administration, with the apparatus of the Zulu state grafted over the top. The regional chiefs – the so-called *izikhulu* (sing. *isikhulu*), or 'great ones' of the nation – were entitled to sit on the *ibandla* or national council which advised the king; so powerful was the *ibandla* that it could – and sometimes did – oppose the king's wishes, and the king could only take direct action against an *isikhulu* at the risk of alienating his support in the outlying areas. Thus effective administration of the Zulu kingdom was the result of a careful balancing act, characterised by an underlying tension between the king's need to centralise power and the regional chiefs' desire to see power revert to them.

Military and political systems

One significant force for centralisation was the military system. In the pre-Shakan clans it had been common for young men to give a period of service to their chiefs, until such time as they married and assumed family responsibilities. Shaka extended this system so that the young men from across the kingdom gave service directly to the king, rather than to their local chiefs, regardless of their regional allegiances. This effectively concentrated the single most obvious military and economic resource directly in the king's hands, and provided one of the strongest bonds tying the nation together. Making use of existing structures, Shaka called young men together by means of guilds called *amabutho* (sing. *ibutho*) which were recruited on the grounds of their common age. The *amabutho* were expected to provide service for the king whenever he demanded it over a period of 15 or even 20 years; at the end of that time, they were allowed to marry and disperse, although the king might still call upon them in extreme circumstances.

King Shaka was probably able to exert a tighter control over his subjects than any of his successors simply because there were no viable alternative political systems within his orbit. Even before his assassination, in 1828, however, the first white adventurers had arrived on the

kingdom was born, largely through the military skills of one of the most important and controversial figures in black southern African history, King Shaka kaSenzangakhona.

So much myth has accrued about the life and times of King Shaka that it is actually quite difficult to discern the thread of truth which links his achievements. He came to power about 1816, and was, it is generally agreed, an aggressive individual who gained a fierce reputation in his youth as a warrior. He is credited with two crucial military innovations: the invention of a broad-bladed spear for use in hand-to-hand combat, and the creation of a deadly battlefield tactic, the 'beast's horns' encircling formation. It is apparently on the strength of these that the Zulu began their ascendancy. Certainly the Zulu rise was rapid; they steadily overcame other contenders for regional dominance, and by about 1820 a recognisable Zulu kingdom had emerged. Its heartland lay between the Black

Zulu borders, and had established a trading settlement at Port Natal (now Durban). Shaka's successor, King Dingane, effectively abandoned the area south of the Thukela River – which was known to Europeans as Natal – to the whites. Throughout the 1830s Natal's black population increased dramatically as refugees from the Zulu kingdom 'crossed over', either fleeing political friction or simply freeing themselves from the more irksome aspects of the obligations imposed by the *amabutho* system. The full repercussions of this drain in resources became apparent in 1838, when the arrival of a new element upset the balance still further, and led to the first direct conflict between the Zulu kingdom and the emerging settler-state in Natal. In that year, Boer farmers – the descendants of the original European settlers at the Cape – arrived in Natal, trekking away from the newly established British

regime there. Hungry for land, they presented a direct challenge to the Zulu kingdom, and a brutal war broke out. It was only resolved in 1840 when King Dingane was overthrown by his brother, Mpande kaSenzangakhona, with Boer help. The Boers claimed a huge reward for helping Mpande, but the Zulu kingdom was spared the full cost by the timely arrival of the British who, exercising a prior claim to Natal, sent troops in 1842 to drive the Boers out. The British formally claimed Natal as a colony, and the boundary between it and the Zulu kingdom was fixed as the Thukela river.

The struggles of 1838–40 seriously weakened the internal position of the Zulu king, as the regional *izikhulu* traded their support for increased regional autonomy. King Mpande's reign was characterised by a struggle to restore the power of the monarchy in the face of internal

Two Zulu boys, of about cadet-age, in 'dancing costume', pictured next to a grain store, by the artist Angas in the 1840s. (British Museum Collection)

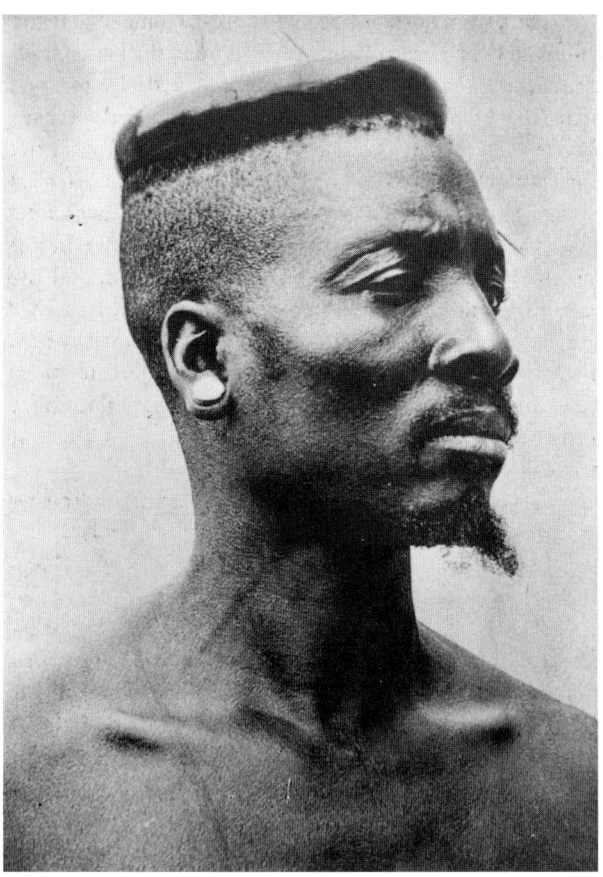

A Zulu man wearing the isicoco head-ring, the sign of a married man which symbolised full adult status. It was a common practice to shave the head around the ring, like this.

army had been defeated, the centres of royal authority destroyed, and the king himself driven from the throne.

However, the framework of the old military system continued to dominate the minds of the Zulu people throughout the remainder of the 19th century – a time of bitter internecine strife between those who wanted the king's power restored and those who were opposed to it and welcomed a neo-colonial system. The royalist faction never succeeded in reuniting the nation, however, and the short-lived royalist rebellion was suppressed by British redcoats in 1888. In 1906 a rebellion directed against the more obvious symbols of Colonial rule – notably taxation – began in Natal, and gained some support amongst adherents of the old Zulu kingdom in the border regions. It was, however, ruthlessly put down, proving for the final time that the 19th century Zulu military outlook had little to offer in the face of the 20th century quick-firing artillery, Maxim-machine guns and magazine rifles.

CHRONOLOGY

*c.*1790 First conflict between the clan groups in the Zululand area.

*c.*1816 Shaka succeeds as chieftain of the Zulu clan.

*c.*1816–1824 Main period of Zulu expansion, defeating local rivals, incorporating neighbouring groups through alliance or conquest. Emergence of Zulu kingdom.

1824 Arrival of first white adventurers at Port Natal.

1828 Assassination of King Shaka; King Dingane abandons area south of Thukela to whites.

1838 War between Zulus and Boers; successful Zulu attacks on Boer encampments, sacking of settlement of Port Natal, but ends in Zulu defeat at Ncome (Blood) River on 16 December.

1840 King Dingane driven out by his brother Mpande kaSenzangakhona, with Boer help.

1842 British defeat Boers at Port Natal, and take over Natal; Natal/Zulu border established at line of Thukela and Mzinyathi (Buffalo) Rivers.

1856 Civil War in Zululand between rival sons of Mpande, the Princes Cetshwayo and Mbuyazi.

1872/73 Death of King Mpande; accession of Cetshwayo.

1879 Anglo-Zulu War. Main Zulu army is directed against British centre column, and defeats it at Isandlwana on 22 January. Zulu reserve is checked in mopping-up operation at Rorke's Drift the same day. Zulu forces on coast defeated at Nyezane. British coastal column digs in at Eshowe. Zulu army reassembled in March to oppose Eshowe

dissent and the lure of an easier life in Colonial Natal. He was partially successful, in so far as the kingdom retained its independence and cohesion despite a damaging civil war in 1856 between two of his heirs. This succession crisis was so severe that even after Mpande's death (1872) his heir, Cetshwayo, remained sufficiently insecure to ask for Colonial Natal's recognition at his installation a year later. The price of this support would cost the kingdom dear, for it was later used by the British to justify their invasion in 1879.

The kingdom held together quite well throughout the crisis of 1879. Only two *izikhulu* defected to the British – one a white protégé of King Cetshwayo – and the army took to the field time and again in defence of its homeland and way of life. On several occasions, notably at Isandlwana on 22 January, it severely defeated British troops in the field, but in the end the Zulu army's reliance on mass attacks in the open made it acutely vulnerable to the effects of British military technology, and it withered in the face of concentrated firepower. By July 1879 the relief column and left flank column; Zulus defeated at Khambula on 28 March and Gingindlovu on 2 April. British advance continues; Zulu army reassembles but is defeated at oNdini (Ulundi) on 4 July. Army dispersed. King captured in August and taken into captivity. British divide Zululand into 13 chiefdoms.

1881   Violence begins between chiefs; first stages in civil war between royalist and anti-royalist factions.

1883/84 King Cetshwayo restored to part of former kingdom; violence intensifies. Cetshwayo defeated and dies. Royalists recruit Boer help to defeat their enemies.

1887   Zululand annexed by Britain.

1888   Royalist rebellion. Cetshwayo's successor, King Dinuzulu, defeated and exiled.

1906/7 Bambatha Rebellion in Natal spreads to Zulu borders but is ruthlessly suppressed.

RECRUITMENT

The Zulu military system was firmly rooted in social practices of the Zulu-speaking peoples which pre-dated it by generations. The Zulu warrior was not a professional, full-time soldier living in the world of a self-contained, self-regulating institution; he remained, essentially, a civilian, upon whom the state imposed the duty to serve in a military capacity when circumstances demanded. The nature of that service changed little from the time of King Shaka to the collapse of the army, in 1879.

The vast majority of people in pre-Colonial Natal and Zululand lived in social units centred upon the homestead, *umuzi* (pl. *imizi*). Each homestead consisted of a married man (the homestead-head or *umnumzana*) and perhaps three or four wives. The homestead was ruled by a strict social hierarchy which found expression in its physical layout: it consisted of a number of neat dome-shaped huts of wattle and thatch, arranged in a circle, with the hut of the chief wife at the top, opposite the entrance, and the remaining huts arranged in order of precedence on either side. In the centre of each *umuzi* was a cattle-pen, where the *umnumzana*'s herd (representing his wealth and status as well as a source of food) were kept at night. The entire homestead was surrounded by a stout palisade to keep out predatory wildlife.

In theory each homestead was self-sufficient, drawing the staple food – milk-curds called *amasi* – from its herds and growing mealies and pumpkins in fields nearby. Most utensils were produced within the homestead, the principle exception being iron, which was made by specialist artisans from clans whose geographic locations provided wood for fuel as well as a plentiful supply of surface deposits of iron ore. There was a strict sexual division of labour: the men supervised the all-important tasks concerned with the care of their stock, and the women supplied the hard physical labour necessary to work the fields. Each homestead acknowledged itself as belonging to a wider grouping, which traced its descent from a supposed common ancestor, and recognised the line of a dominant family as a hereditary chief. The true Zulus believed they were the descendants of a man named Zulu, whose adherents had taken the name *amaZulu* (Zulu's people) or *abakwaZulu* (those of Zulu's place).

The ikhanda: a model of King Cetshwayo's oNdini homestead, showing the fenced-off isigodlo area at the top and the huts occupied by warriors on either side. (Zulu Cultural Museum, oNdini)

7

Rites of passage

A man born into this society would discover, as he grew up, that each stage of his development was recognised by protective rituals. The Zulu-speaking peoples believed in the existence of an afterlife, populated by generations of ancestral spirits, which at times overlapped the everyday life of the living; almost every misfortune that occurred was thought to be the result of a disequilibrium between the two, and great care was taken on all important occasions to appease the ancestral spirits and prevent the spiritual contamination which resulted from their wrath. Life for Zulus of both sexes was a succession of rites of passage, and each stage brought new rights and responsibilities. Unmarried children were considered subordinate to their parents, and had little freedom of action; they were expected to serve and respect their elders, in gratitude for their birth, upbringing and keep. Only when they married did they move out of their parents' home, establish their own *imizi*, and achieve the full independence implied by adult status. This obligation to serve authority provided the psychological framework for the Zulu army.

For perhaps the first five or six years of his life, the Zulu boy had a carefree existence, living in his mother's hut, and playing with other children within the homestead. Once he was considered old enough to be entrusted into the care of older boys, however, he became a herd-boy, tending first goats and sheep and then the cattle. Since cattle were of immense importance in the Zulu world – an exchange of cattle was crucial to the marriage contract, and cattle represented independence, wealth and status, as well as providing a means of sacrifice to the spirits and the physical security of food and hides – this was a very important position. Cattle were driven out early in the morning, and the herd-boys had to keep them safe from accidents and predators, and prevent them from straying into the fields and damaging the crops. Life as a herd-boy taught the young Zulu the rudiments of the discipline he would need in his military life: to respect the authority of those older than himself; to be responsible; to be self-reliant and yet function within a group; and to be familiar with the outdoor environment.

Although young Zulu boys were discouraged from playing with spears, their games had an essentially military nature. This was inevitable in a male-dominated society which defined masculinity in terms of physical courage, and where all Zulu men needed to carry weapons for self-protection against attack and wild animals. From an early age, Zulu boys carried sticks, with which they learned to hunt and to settle differences with one another (in duels

Part of King Cetshwayo's reconstructed oNdini homestead, showing huts built over the surviving clay floors. These huts are typical both of those in the amakhanda *and those in the private homesteads about the country.*

A contemporary sketch of the oNdini homestead, which included over a thousand huts. Few amakhanda *were quite as big as this; most consisted of between 100 and 300 huts.*

fought according to set rules and conditions). Birds and rabbits were caught using throwing sticks with a bulbous knob at one end; and a popular game involved throwing sharpened sticks at a rolling tuber called an *insema*. The boys would form two lines on a slope, and the *insema* would be tossed between them, bouncing down the slope. Each boy would throw his stick at the tuber as it passed, and the winner was the one who succeeded in transfixing it most thoroughly. In a stick fight, each contestant had two straight sticks, one held about midway in the left hand, for parrying, and the other held in the right, for striking. Each contestant would try to land a blow on his opponent, using the stick in his left hand as a shield. Fights were fast and furious, although generally good natured; anyone losing his temper was in any case liable to be at a serious disadvantage against a cool opponent. The fight ended when one contestant struck the head of the other and drew blood, and as a gesture of reconciliation the victor was expected to help wash the loser's wounds.

From about the age of 11 or 12, the Zulu boy would also be expected to fulfil another occasional duty. Whenever his father or any of his elder brothers who were already enrolled in the military system were summoned to undertake a journey, perhaps to attend the king, the young herd-boy who have to accompany him as his carrier and servant. Known as *izindibi* (sing. *udibi*), they were responsible for carrying their senior's head-rest, drinking gourd, food and skin-cloak, all wrapped up in a sleeping mat. All journeys, of course, took place on foot, and the travellers might easily cover 20 miles a day. One of the famous legends about Shaka tells of how he made his warriors discard their hide sandals and go about barefoot; whether this is true or not, the Zulu were certainly barefoot when the first white adventurers encountered them in the 1820s, and they remained so until European clothing became commonplace, in the 20th century. White travellers noted with some fascination that most Zulus had developed a hard layer of horny skin to protect the soles of their feet. All of this travelling was undertaken in a country which had no roads, and still teemed with dangerous wildlife; although Zulu customs of hospitality were such that any traveller could claim a hut and food for the night, journeys remained potentially hazardous. The young *udibi* learned stamina, how to cope in a dangerous environment, and something of the world outside the immediate confines of his homestead. In particular, it was probably at such an age that he first encountered the obvious symbols of the Zulu state – the royal homesteads known as *amakhanda* (sing. *ikhanda*).

Male dress at its most minimal – the umncedo.

THE *AMAKHANDA*

The *amakhanda* – the word translates literally as 'heads' – were centres for the dissemination of royal authority. Physically, they were built much like ordinary *imizi*, but on a grander scale; most *amakhanda* contained 200–300 huts; and the principal ones, where the king himself spent most of his time, boasted more than 1,000. They were arranged in a circle, around a central enclosure which served as both a parade ground for the warriors quartered there and a pen for the royal cattle. At the top of each *ikhanda* was a fenced-off area known as the *isigodlo*, which was the king's private quarters when he was in residence. Although each of the kings had a favourite residence – known as the *komkhulu*, or 'great place' – most of them travelled frequently among the *amakhanda*, and each was considered his personal property. They were built at strategic points about the kingdom, to serve as a layer of state administration alongside the local administration of the district chiefs. Shaka is thought to have had perhaps 13 or 14 *amakhanda*; this grew to 27 in Cetshwayo's time – 13 of them within sight of each other on the Mahlabathini plain, in the very heart of the kingdom – according to a careful count by the British intelligence department on the eve of the 1879 war.

The *amakhanda* served as barracks for the Zulu regiments when they were mustered for service. As a result, when the regiments were not in residence, but living at their family homesteads, an *ikhanda* might house only a handful of people – members of the king's household and a caretaker complement of warriors. When the regiments were mustered, however, there would be four or five warriors sharing each hut.

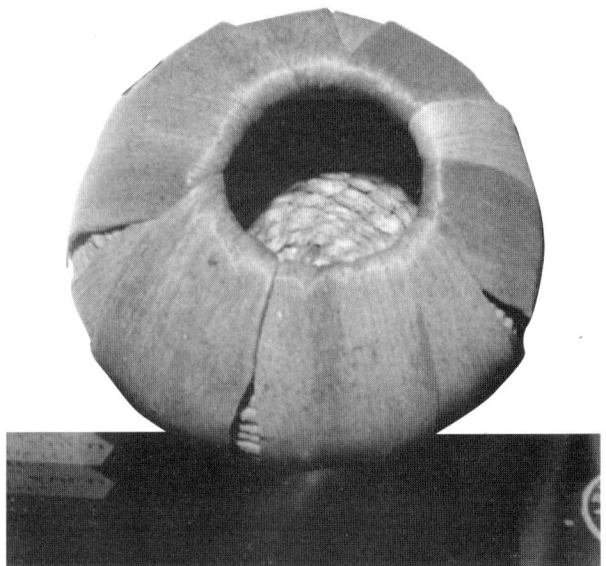

To some extent a warrior was dependent on his family for food in an ikhanda; here Zulu girls have brought fresh pumpkins. The grass rings (bottom right) were worn as a pad when carrying things on the head, and are known as inkatha.

When an *udibi* boy accompanied a relative to an *ikhanda*, his first duty was to clean out the hut, which may have been empty for some time. He was then expected to fetch and carry, for which he received no reward other than a share in the warriors' food. Indeed, he was probably subject to some heavy-handed horseplay; in the confused warren of huts, he might get lost, and if he entered the wrong hut he could expect to have a bone thrown at him, or be given a clip round the ear and told to take care.

At the end of his relative's visit to the *ikhanda*, the *udibi* returned home and resumed his duties as a herd-boy. This pattern characterised the life of a Zulu warrior throughout the period of the kingdom's existence. Since in theory every Zulu man was expected to fulfil the role of warrior in his turn, the Zulu army was therefore nothing less than the manpower of the nation, assembled and mobilised for war.

JOINING A REGIMENT

Amabutho framework

It seems to have been up to the individual to determine when they entered service to the stak. Every Zulu child, male and female, belonged to an age-group, called an *intanga* (pl. *izintanga*), simply by virtue of having been born in a particular three- or four-year period. Each homestead probably produced two or three children who fell within an *intanga*, and they would play together from early childhood. The *intanga* extended to neighbouring

homesteads, the chiefdom and, ultimately, the kingdom as a whole. These *izintanga* formed the basis of the *amabutho* system; both males and females were formed into *amabutho*, although female *amabutho* were largely an administrative convenience. It was unusual for them to be called together – a woman might be a member of a particular *ibutho* all her life, and never meet fellow members outside her immediate locality – and they had no particular duties; they did, however, serve as a useful counterpart for male *amabutho* when the latter were allowed to marry.

The *Inkwebane*

When a Zulu youth reached the age of 17 or 18, he decided to go, apparently of his own volition and sometimes despite the opposition of his father, to report to the nearest *ikhanda* to *kleza*. The term *kleza* means to drink milk straight from the cow's udder, and it was meant literally as well as figuratively, for young men would be sustained by milk from the king's herds, and offer him service in return. Here he would meet other youths of the same group who had gathered to offer service for the king. They were known as *inkwebane*, and were in effect cadet warriors. Their duties were not particularly harsh, and varied from learning the basics of Zulu fighting techniques to performing the king's chores. They tended the royal cattle, helped keep the homestead in repair, and hoed nearby mealie fields. They practised stick-fighting, and may have undertaken occasional runs across country to build their endurance. On the whole, most Zulus who experienced it seemed to enjoy their time as a cadet rather more than they had as an *udibi*; the work was less onerous, and the bonds of fellowship they formed would provide the framework for the full-fledged regimental *esprit de corps* which came later. The period of cadetship perhaps lasted three or four years, and it is not clear whether the boys lived in the *amakhanda* for all that time; they were probably allowed frequent time off to visit their families and take part in important ceremonies at home.

The *Inkwebane* were supervised in their cadetship by *izinduna* (sing. *induna*) attached to the royal homesteads. The *izinduna* were a layer of administration imposed over the clan structure - state functionaries, appointed by the king, to act as administrators, military commanders and messengers, or to fulfil other specific duties. They were not necessarily men of hereditary rank – indeed, some of the Zulu kings appear to have preferred to raise up men whose status in civilian life was otherwise limited, since they then owed their position directly to the king himself. Often, however, the most important posts were occupied by men of the highest rank; the king's military command-

The head-ring of a married man was closely bound into the hair, and could only be removed when the hair itself was cut away, as, apparently, with this example. (Natal Museum)

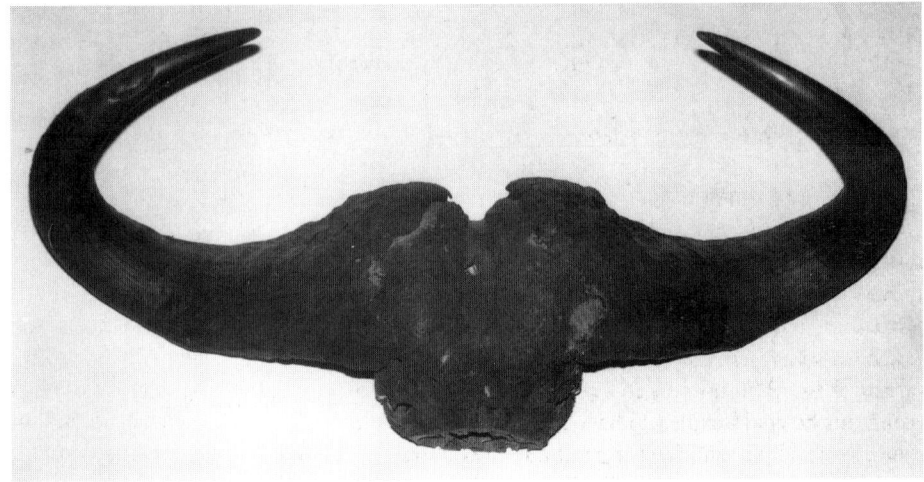

The 'beast's horns', the Zulu attack formation, was said to resemble a charging bull, and these buffalo horns suggest something of the symbolism. The 'chest' provides the main thrust, while the 'horns' rush out on either side. (SB Bourquin).

ers were usually chosen from among the most trusted *izikhulu* who sat on the *ibandla* council.

In addition to the *izinduna*, each *ikhanda* was usually under the care of a senior and venerated female member of the royal household. Because of the system of polygamy, there were a large number of royal queens within the kingdom, including the widows of the previous monarch. It was impossible – and socially unwise – to house them together, and they were usually placed in charge of the king's quarters in each of the *amakhanda*. They supervised the running of the *isigodlo*, and kept a watchful eye on the *isigodlo* girls, the king's female attendants.

Zulu society respected both age and authority, but it was as a cadet that the Zulu youth probably encountered authority in all its most awe-inspiring forms. Young men were, in any case, expected to respect their elders – to get out of their way, for example, if they met them on the path – and if at some time a cadet encountered the king, he would regard him almost with dread, not only because any accidental breech of etiquette might incur disgrace or even instant death, but because the king's person was held to be the receptacle of the accumulated power of the royal

family's ancestral spirits. Ordinarily, commoners dared not look him in the face, and his anger was so great that, according to one delightful account, even *izikhulu* 'would look shamefaced, and cast down their eyes . . . Their penis-covers would fall off'. This awe pervaded the state system, since the hereditary chiefs and state officials both carried with them some reflection of the king's status. For the most part, however, the physical expression of this author-ity was limited; the Zulu warrior lived under no book of military law, simply because the same laws were common to all aspects of Zulu life. Serious crimes – notably interfering in the supernatural world to cause another harm, or insulting in some way the king's majesty – were punishable by death, but the *izinduna* commonly exerted their authority by means of the stick. Any minor lapse in duty was punished by a beating, administered on the spot and soon forgotten; it was apparently a common expres-sion among the warriors that 'we never can hear, unless we first feel the stick'.

When the king decided that there were enough cadets gathered together around the kingdom, he called them to his great place to *buta* them (enrol them as a regiment), a ceremony which seems to have been quite simple, and involved the king giving them a formal name, and ordering them to establish their own *ikhanda* at an appointed spot. Generally, therefore, each *ibutho* had its own *ikhanda*, but occasionally regiments were drafted into existing units to maintain strength. This didn't usually cause a problem if the regiments were of a similar age – in the 1870s, for example, the *uVe ibutho* was incorporated on formation with the iNgobamakhosi, the *ibutho* whose formation had immediately preceded it – but occasionally regiments put into the same *ikhanda* varied considerably in age. This could lead to conflict, since, despite the highly developed structure of Zulu society, there were inter-generational tensions. Older men were protective of their experience and status, while young men resented being excluded from the world of wives and cattle, and felt themselves to be better soldiers. At the first fruits ceremony in late 1877, when the young iNgobamakhosi were ordered to share the huts of King Cetshwayo's great place – oNdini (Ulundi) – with the older uThulwana, a clash occurred. A stick fight broke out, and the commander of the uThulwana was so

furious at the disrespect shown by the 'boys' of the iNgobamakhosi that he ordered his men to arm themselves with spears, with the result that a significant number of men were killed.

Stick fights were, indeed, a common occurrence when several of the *amabutho* were gathered together, particularly in the heady atmosphere of one of the big national festivals. The common age of the warriors and their shared experience meant that they tended to forge strong bonds, with the result that the *amabutho* were highly competitive with one another. When a regiment was *buta*'d, the cadets would meet, for the first time, their counterparts from other parts of the kingdom – young men who acknowledged different local chiefs and many of whom followed slightly different practices or had regional accents. Nevertheless, being joined together in the service of the king was a bond so powerful that many men referred to themselves by their regimental names rather than by their clan names. To outsiders, they described themselves as Zulus, because they acknowledged their allegiance to the Zulu king; after their patronym, however, they sometimes called themselves by the name of their *ibutho* rather than by their clan name. Thus a man named Xhawulisa, the son of Sipho, of, say, the Cube clan, who was a member of the iNgobamakhosi, might describe himself as a Zulu, but call himself Xhawulisa kaSipho iNgobamakhosi or Xhawulisa kaSipho Cube. This sense of pride in belonging to a particular group was easily channelled by the *amabutho* system into a specifically military pride. Rivalries between regiments were deliberately encouraged by the Zulu kings, since they could be used to good effect on the battlefield.

CONDITIONS OF SERVICE

Having been *buta*'d by the king, the newly enrolled regiment could expect to spend several months building its *ikhanda*, but would then probably be allowed to disperse. It is generally believed that Shaka kept his army permanently mobilised, but this is unlikely, given that the young men had to be provisioned and kept busy when they were in the *amakhanda*, and this would have been difficult for long periods. In fact, even Shaka probably allowed them to return to their homes and resume their civilian lives. When the king needed them, they were summoned, and

A young warrior in full ceremonial dress, including a leopardskin head-band, amaphovela, *and a profusion of cow-* *tails around the body. The shield is the large* isihlangu *type and is typically black. (Royal Archives)*

were expected to report to their *ikhanda* without delay.

Although the *amabutho* functioned most obviously as an army, this was only one of their roles; they were also the state labour force, keeping the king's homesteads in good repair and tending his cattle, and the internal police-force, punishing wrong-doers on the king's orders. They also took part in the nation's important religious rites, including the ceremonial hunts which were required to cleanse the kingdom after some important event – the so-called 'washing of the spears'. For the most part, the average Zulu warrior would have spent more time in these mundane duties than he would in the short, sharp bursts of campaigning that characterised Zulu warfare. He might expect to be called up three or four times in a year, for perhaps a month or two at a time. Call-up duties included the *umKhosi* ceremony, the annual festival to usher in the first fruits of the season, which took place in December or January, and which served as the grand review of the entire army.

Social activities

Life in the *amakhanda* was not particularly hard. The warriors slept on grass mats on the hard clay floor, resting their heads on carved wooden head-rests, and using a soft animal-skin as a blanket. The hut had a fireplace in the centre of the floor, but no chimney, so it was permanently smoky; this did at least help reduce insect infestation in the thatch. They were, however, probably plagued by rats and mice, who ran over them at night, scavenging for crumbs of food, but they would have been used to this from birth. The hut was dry in rainy weather and cool on a hot day, and if they were lucky, they might have the services of an *udibi*.

The Zulus ate twice a day – at mid-morning and in the evening – and when living in the *amakhanda*, the men were largely dependent on the king's bounty for food. They received no pay for their service, but the king was obliged to feed them, and the staple diet consisted of beef and sorghum beer. Since beef was only eaten on special occasions ordinarily – cattle were far too valuable to be slaughtered for meat alone – the warrior probably ate more of it when serving the king than at any other time in his life. The king or his *izinduna* picked out a few head of cattle each day, and these were slaughtered; the meat was distributed to various communal kitchens about the *amakhanda*, then boiled and distributed. The means of cooking were fairly basic, and the meat was often tough, and took a good deal of chewing before it could be swallowed; one European visitor commented that meal-times were characterised by the sound of mass chewing which hung over an *ikhanda* like the sighing of the wind.

The king also provided beer called *utshwala*, which was brewed from sorghum, and had a thick, creamy consistency and a rather sour taste. Rich in nutrients, it provided an appropriate accompaniment to the meat, and was only mildly intoxicating. Drunkenness was not unknown, but it did require persistence and the ability to consume large quantities of liquid! For variety, the warriors were sometimes supplied with vegetables brought to

A warrior in the typical costume of a married ibutho: *head-ring, otter-skin head-band, and crane feathers. The shield carried here is the smaller* ihawu *type, rather than a regimental war-shield, which would presumably have been white. (Royal Collection)*

A group of men photographed in full regalia at the end of the 19th century. Although they are not in the service of the Zulu kings, their costume and shields are typical of the pre-1879 amabutho. (Natal Archives)

the *amakhanda* by their sisters. This was convenient if a man's family homestead was near his barracks, but less so if it was so far away that his relatives were discouraged from making the journey. Indeed, although the early kings – Shaka and Dingane – were said to be generous with their cattle, there are suggestions that in the latter days of the kingdom there was a serious shortage of food – leading to real hunger in the *amakhanda*. This may have been due in part to the economic decline which followed the civil war of 1840, the rise of colonial Natal, and the spread of several serious bovine diseases; certainly both Mpande and Cetshwayo seem to have suffered something of a crisis of resources. Whatever the reason, the supply of food to the *amakhanda* seems to have been unpredictable in the 1870s, and there are even stories of men dying of starvation.

Routine in the *amakhanda* seems to have revolved around food-times and the need to perform domestic duties. When the warriors were required, the order was given, 'Let the regiments assemble', and the warriors streamed out of their huts and formed up in the central cattle-pen. If the king was in residence, it was here that he inspected them. (He did not always walk among them, but

sometimes merely watched from a mound which allowed him to look over the fence of the *isigodlo*.) There was little in the way of formal drill, although Shaka is said to have organised mock contests between different groups of warriors armed with reeds. One hurled their reeds like throwing spears, whilst the other charged down on them, using theirs as stabbing spears; at the moment of impact the charging party bowled over several of the 'throwers', and the effectiveness of hand-to-hand fighting was duly demonstrated.

It is not clear whether any formal weapon training was given; most Zulu men were used to handling spears in their daily lives, although some combat techniques were preferred over others. For the most part, however, military exercises consisted of carefully choreographed dancing displays. These taught a warrior how to undertake complex manoeuvres without breaking ranks, how to maintain formation, and how to respond quickly to whistles or shouts of command. The adventurer Nathanial Isaacs described a dance he witnessed at King Shaka's *komkhulu*, kwaBulawayo, in terms which clearly indicate its underlying military purpose:

'They formed a circle; the men in the centre and the boys at the two extremities. The king placed himself in the middle of the space within the circle, and about 1,500 girls stood opposite to the men, three deep, in a straight line, and with great

regularity. His majesty then commenced dancing, the warriors followed, and the girls kept time by singing, clapping their hands, and raising their bodies on their toes. The strange attitudes of the men exceeded anything I had seen before. The king was remarkable for his unequalled activity, and the surprising muscular powers he exhibited . . . This ceremony was performed with considerable regularity, from the king giving, as it were, the time for every motion. Wherever he cast his eye, there was the greatest effort made; and nothing could exceed the exertion of the whole until sunset . . .'

Such displays often went on into the evening, and were regarded as a recreation in themselves. For the most part, the Zulu warrior relaxed by gossiping with his fellows over the beer-pot and taking snuff. Snuff was carried in various containers of bone or horn, and its consumption was a social act, as it was considered courteous for friends to pass it round. It was also common for older men to smoke cannabis from a smoking horn, or *igudu*.

Objections to the Zulu system

Since the process of enlistment into the *amabutho* was such a natural one, exceptions were rare. It was not compulsory for a youth to go up to *kleza*, but the practice was so ingrained that it took an exceptional man to object. Anyone failing to enlist was likely to be regarded as a coward, and this damaged his reputation in the eyes of potential suitors. For such men life within the Zulu kingdom had

little to offer, and those who refused to *kleza* had little option but to 'cross over' into Natal. Indeed, the generally easier conditions in Natal, where the chiefs required no highly developed tribute of service, and it was much easier for a young man to marry, accounted for most defections. A few men simply objected to the hardy lifestyle of the warrior – the lack of food, the danger of being provoked into a stick-fight or the prospect of a disciplinary beating – but these were a minority, as most of these hazards were not unique to military life. Young men who felt themselves touched by the spirit world, and who felt themselves called as either an *inyanga* (a herbalist doctor) or a *sangoma* (a diviner) were freed from the obligation to serve in the *amabutho*. However, when King Mpande suspected that too many were taking this option, he called them all together and grafted them to an *ibutho* he was about to *buta*. The later kings also allowed regiments to marry rather earlier than Shaka had done, and both Mpande and Cetshwayo maintained *amabandla mhlope* – white assemblies – consisting of regiments which had been allowed to marry but which still mustered in the *amakhanda* to serve the king, often taking their wives with them. These measures were an attempt to undercut the reasons for defection, and certainly had some success, especially as life under Colonial rule came to seem less and less attractive.

A group of warriors in full regalia. Based on a group who were brought to England in the 1850s as a curiosity.

MARRIAGE

Marriage was perhaps the most crucial rite of passage in Zulu society, and it had profound implications for a man's civilian and military life. Until a man married, he was considered an *insizwa*, a youth, whatever his age; he belonged to his father's household, and his individual rights and responsibilities were strictly limited. When he married, however, he became an *indoda*, a man; he moved out of his father's homestead, and assumed all of the privileges of an *umnumzana*. His first loyalty was no longer to his father or the state, but to his immediate family and, by extension, his local chief.

This practice had important consequences for the *amabutho* system, since it meant, in effect, that when a man married, he passed out of the king's control. He was no longer available for immediate call-up, and could not be asked to spend long periods in the *amakhanda*. In other words, marriage inevitably marked the end of the period of active service, and was the point when a warrior passed onto the semi-retired list.

Shaka sought to balance this by artificially delaying the onset of the first marriage. In the Zulu system, it was necessary for the king to grant permission for the *amabutho* to marry, and Shaka simply refused to do so until the last possible moment. This maximised his resources while at the same time undercutting the authority of the regional chiefs by denying them the return of their manpower. As a consequence, some *amabutho* were not allowed to marry until the men reached their mid-forties, although this was not as uncomfortable for them as it might sound, since Zulu society acknowledged various forms of pre-marital sexual activity, so long as it did not result in pregnancy. (The Victorian picture of hordes of young warriors seething with a sexual frustration somehow transmuted to bloodlust was a lurid and distorted image which probably says more about contemporary British sexual repression than it does Zulu culture.) Nevertheless, the men clearly resented this delay – a prolonged exclusion from the world of cattle and status. In the reign of the later kings, it proved impossible to delay marriage for so long, since the existence of Colonial Natal across the borders offered an alternative to disgruntled men and women alike. By 1879, most *amabutho* were allowed to marry by their late thirties. By then, a regiment had served for over 15 years, which probably included some campaigning; herein is the origin of the Colonial belief that a regiment was never allowed to marry until it had been blooded in war. There was no direct correlation between the two events, however: King Cetshwayo was quite specific that 'this had nothing to do with the matter'. In fact, the system also allowed the king to have some control over the rate at which the nation reproduced, since the longer female *amabutho* remained unmarried, the shorter their fertility span would be.

King Mpande reviewing an ibutho. One of his attendants holds a shield over him to ward off the sun, and another holds a gourd for drinking. Selected warriors giya – leaping out from the ranks to perform a solitary display of military skill. (SB Bourquin)

Right: The basis of the head-dress, a stuffed otter-skin head-band, with ear-flaps attached. (Natal Museum)

The king usually announced which regiments he was permitting to marry at the annual *umKhosi* ceremony. A male *ibutho* would be told to seek brides from a female guild, usually composed of girls a few years younger. As a sign that they had received royal permission, the young men were allowed to *tunga*, to sew on the headring which marked this important change in status. The ring itself, called *isicoco*, was made by carefully binding a fibre into the hair, then plastering it with a natural gum which had been coloured with charcoal. When dry, the ring was polished with beeswax, and the hair around it shaved, to accentuate its appearance. The ring was sometimes known as 'the king's ring', because it implied a degree of royal approval. Women, too, adopted a physical mark of their new state, teasing up a top-knot on the crown of the head, colouring it with red ochre, and shaving the hair around it. Sporting their new headrings, the warriors then dispersed and sought out girls among the appropriate age-group, and weddings took place individually according to traditional rites.

For the most part the girls accepted this system, although a few chose instead to become the second or third wives of older men who were already married, and who were probably wealthier in cattle. Occasionally, if the girls did object, the consequences could be serious. In 1876, for example, King Cetshwayo allowed the male iNdlondlo *ibutho* to *tunga*, and told them to choose partners from among the female iNgcugce, who were several years younger. Many in the iNgcugce had formed attachments with younger *amabutho*, and commented derisively that 'the string of beads does not meet around the neck', meaning that there were not enough men of the iNdlondlo to go round. The king, determined to check this challenge to his authority, ordered the iNgcugce to marry by a certain date or suffer the consequences. Most obeyed, but a number of girls slipped into Natal; others remained defiant, so the king ordered several to be killed. It proved a salutary lesson, that the structures of state control could not be flouted lightly, but the incident played into the hands of propagandists in Natal, who were already preparing the ground for an armed British intervention in Zulu affairs.

Once a couple had married, they set about establishing a homestead, and raising a family. The man continued to acknowledge his membership of his *ibutho*, but he was only liable to be summoned to the king for the annual *umKhosi* ceremony or for a major campaign. He was therefore largely lost as a resource to the state, and in order to counter this, both Mpande and Cetshwayo maintained *amabandla mhlope* or 'white assemblies' of *amabutho* who were married, and therefore carried white shields, but who still spent time serving in the *amakhanda*. Conditions were much more relaxed for them, and they were allowed to take their wives with them, and could come and go almost at will. In 1879 the main Zulu army included a number of married regiments, including the uThulwana *ibutho* – the main unit present at the attack on Rorke's Drift.

ORGANISATION

The basic pattern for the internal organisation of an *ibutho* was established in cadetship. The cadets were organised into companies, *amaviyo* (sing. *iviyo*), which varied considerably in size, from as few as 50 to as many as 200. The reason for this disparity remains obscure; it may have had something to do with the numbers of youths who reported to each *ikhanda*, but the king himself sometimes tinkered with the structure, drafting extra recruits into some companies which seemed to him understrength. Indeed, it is often difficult to assess the strength of a Zulu force in any given engagement, because the Zulus merely counted the number of companies present. There was no set number of companies per *ibutho*, nor was the strength of an *ibutho* predetermined. In the early days of the kingdom, most *amabutho* seem to have numbered about 900 men, but the units raised in the 1870s were much larger, probably reflecting the success of King Cetshwayo's attempts to revitalise the military system.

Companies who *kleza*'d at a particular *ikhanda* tended

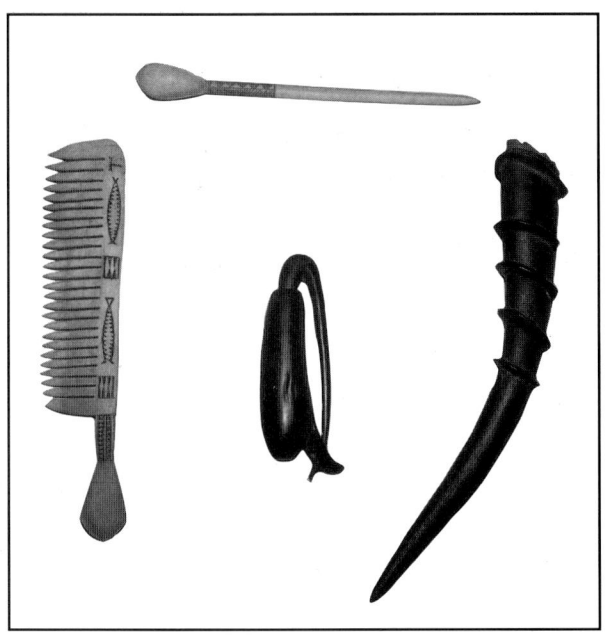

Personal ornamentation: two snuff-spoons (top and left), one combined with a comb, and two containers for snuff. (Natal Museum)

appointed from their ranks, and were administered by *izinduna* attached to the *amakhanda*. Inevitably, however, each *iviyo* produced a number of natural leaders, who by common consent spoke up for their colleagues. Officers were appointed by the king once the regimental *ikhanda* had been built. The regiment would be summoned to the *komkhulu*, and the king's attendants would call out the names of those chosen. For the most part, those who had shown leadership qualities would be confirmed as junior *izinduna*, with command over their companies. Each *isigaba* had an appointed *induna*, and a senior commander and second-in-command were also selected. Almost certainly, the king relied on the reports of *izinduna* who had supervised the regiment in its cadetship when appointing these officers from within the ranks, although the more senior ranks were filled by men selected from the older *amabutho* – men whose abilities were already known to the king.

UNIFORM

When a regiment *buta*'d, the king specified that it should wear a particular uniform of feathers and furs, and carry a shield with a particular colour on the face. The ordinary dress of a Zulu male was minimal: it consisted of a small sheath of bamboo leaves, known as the *umncedo*, worn over the penis. To appear in a public place without the *umncedo* was considered the most appalling breach of manners, but, conversely, a man was thought to be decently dressed in almost all circumstances if he was wearing nothing but an *umncedo*. In fact, however, almost all men wore a loin-covering, known as the *umutsha*, over the top. This con-

to form a sub-unit within the regiment when they were *buta*'d. They were quartered in the same part of their regimental *ikhanda*, and were known as an *isigaba* (pl. *izigaba*) or division. Thus, for example, the uKhandempemvu (uMcijo) *ibutho*, which fought in 1879, had 12 *izigaba* containing a total of 49 companies; according to British sources, it had a total strength of about 2,500 men.

In the cadet phase, the young men had no officers

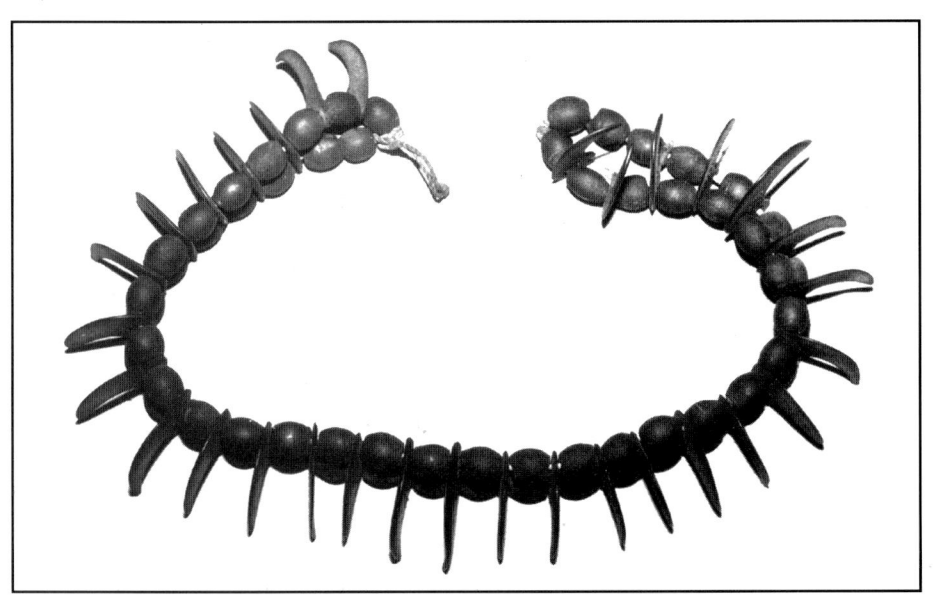

An indication of rank: a necklace of red beads and carved bone 'claws', worn as a symbol of status. (Natal Museum)

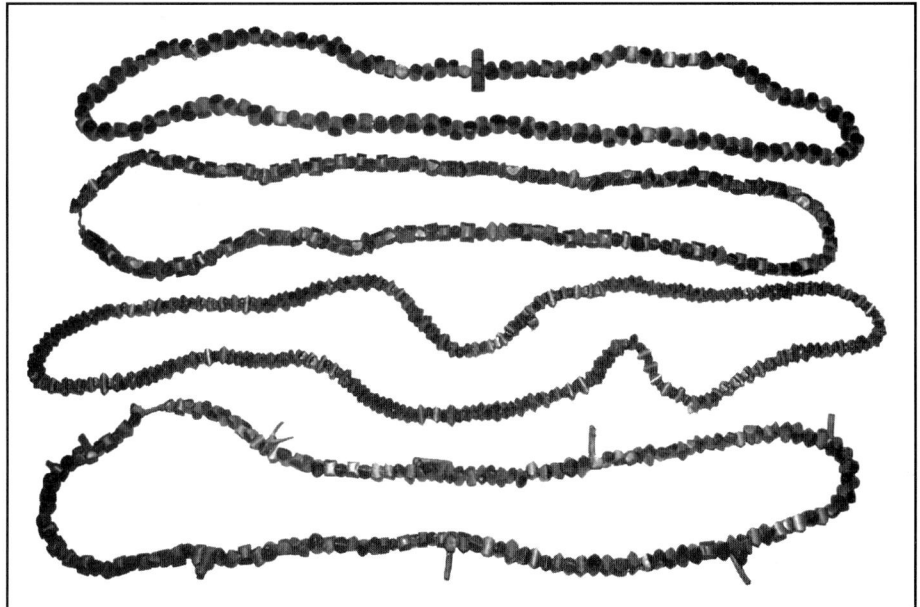

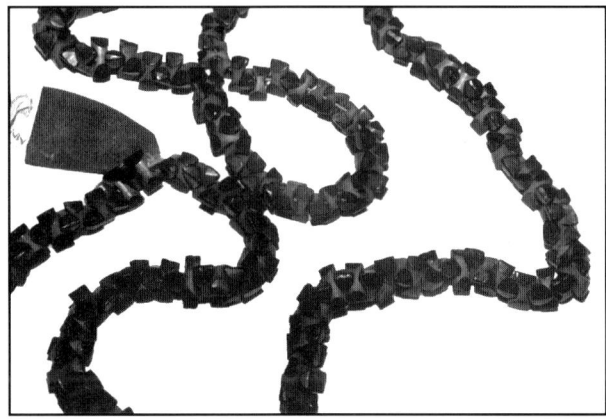

sisted of a thin belt of hide, with a square of soft calf-skin, known as *ibeshu*, over the buttocks, and bunches of animal 'tails' hanging over the front. These tails (*isinene*) were in fact made up of strips of fur, usually of civet, twisted together to resemble tails; two contrasting colours of skin were often used to produce an attractive alternating effect.

Each man provided his own *umutsha*, and it was over this that the regimental dress was worn. Most conspicuous in this was a profusion of cow-tails. These were flayed from the carcass so that each tail consisted of a strip of skin with the long bushy hair attached; they were then tied in bunches to bands which were worn around the arms and legs, or to a leather necklace, so that they hung in a dense mop over the chest and back, as far as the waist at the front and the knees at the back. Almost the entire body was obscured, and white travellers sometimes found it difficult to recognise men they knew well when they were fully dressed.

Such body ornaments were common to all the *amabutho*, although the more senior regiments wore a magnificent kilt or *insimba* of twisted tails which circled right round the waist and hung to the knees. It was in the head-dress, however, that the most striking differences could be seen. The basis of the head-dress was the *umqele*, a padded roll, usually of otter or leopard-skin, stitched into a tube, stuffed with a bull-rush or dried cow-dung, and neatly tied behind the head. Hanging down from the sides were ear-flaps (*amabheqe*) usually of *isamango* or monkey-skin, which sometimes hung as far as the collar-bone. Stuck into the head-band were a variety of feathers which were either tied together or, for more extravagant plumes, fixed to a framework of grass on top of the head. Some feathers carried associations of youth, others of seniority; the tail feathers from the breeding plumage of the long-tailed widow bird (*sakabuli*) were tied in bunches to porcupine quills and usually fixed on either side of the head as part of the costume of unmarried regiments, while the tail feathers of the blue crane (*indwe*) were worn singly or in pairs by senior regiments. Ostrich feathers were worn in some profusion and in a variety of combinations, so that the contrast between the long white feathers and shorter black feathers was carefully stressed. Other feathers were worn according to the king's dictates – perhaps a clipped ball of feathers over the forehead, or a large bunch floating gracefully behind the head. One characteristic of the dress of the younger *amabutho* were *amaphovela* – two strips of stiff cow-hide which were bound across the forehead so as to rise up over the temples, with cow-tails attached to the tips.

For the most part, lavish costume was only worn on

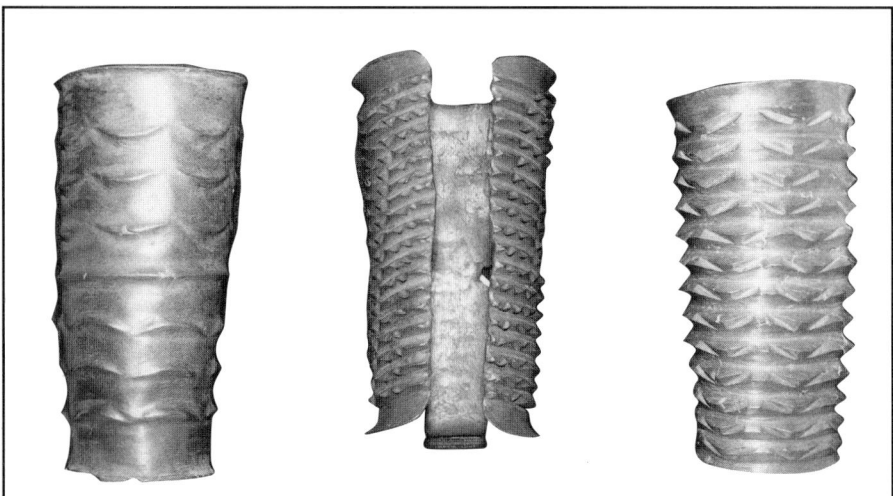

Izingxotha, the brass arm-bands awarded by the Zulu kings to men of the highest rank for outstanding service to the state. (Natal Museum)

ceremonial occasions, notably at the annual *umKhosi* cere-mony. For one thing, some of it was uncomfortable – the heavy cow-tail necklaces chafed the neck, for example – and for another, it was fragile and expensive. Henry Fynn estimated that the *insimba* alone 'generally contain from 15 to 20 skins in a dress, sometimes 50 or 60, putting an astonishing value on them', and the number of skins and feathers needed to costume an army in excess of 20,000 men was staggering. Some of this costume was provided by the king himself; it came from material presented to him as tribute. In particular, the Tsonga groups who lived on the northern Zululand coast, around St. Lucia Bay, and who acknowledged the authority of the Zulu king were regularly called upon to provide hundreds of pelts. Most were distributed by the king to the *amabutho*. Although the exact mechanisms are obscure, the evidence suggests that the king distributed a number of items to an *ibutho* when he enrolled it, and perhaps later if the costume was in any way altered. There were not enough pelts or feathers to go round, and most of them probably went to the *izilomo* (warriors who were known to the king and who achieved considerable status by virtue of his favour). Enough were given, however, to start the regiment off, and as an indication of the uniform expected of them. It was then left to the warriors to procure the rest them-selves, presumably by trading on their own account. When full regalia was worn, it was important that the individual warriors were well turned out, since to appear badly dressed before the king was considered a disgrace. The costumes of the various *amabutho* were well-known, and any man not wearing his properly was liable to be mocked or beaten.

Some elements were particularly indicative of rank. Only *izikhulu* or their sons were allowed to wear leopard-skins in any quantity; if a commoner killed a leopard, he was required to send the carcass or skin to his chief. It was sometimes worn around the shoulders by important men, with the tail falling down over the stomach. The feathers of the scarlet lourie might only be worn by *izinduna* or by men favoured by the king. Other such symbols of rank included a necklace made from dark red beads, inter-spersed with carefully carved chips of bone, made to look like leopard-claws.

SHIELDS

The ceremonial regalia worn by the regiments were con-sidered to be part of the king's bounty – part of the web of patronage and obligation that bound the army to his service. Similarly, the regimental war-shields were not the property of the individual, but rather of the king. Every Zulu man had a number of shields for his everyday use, for a variety of specific purposes: small shields for courting or dancing, and a larger shield, the *ihawu*, for personal protection. These he kept in his hut in his family home-stead, but the war-shields belonged to the state, and were kept in the *amakhanda*, and only issued to the *amabutho* when they were mustered. The largest war-shield, the *isihlangu*, was about 54 in. by 30 in. in Shaka's day, and although such huge shields were still in use in 1879, smaller variants were more common. Most *isihlangu* shields dating from 1879 were about 47 in. by 27 in. In the 1850s, during the civil war between the princes Cetshwayo and Mbuyazi, Cetshwayo introduced an even smaller type, called the *umbumbuluzo*. It averaged 40 in. by 20 in., and was the most popular type carried in 1879.

All shields were made of cowhide, and were oval in shape, the big *isihlangu* type being slightly more pointed at either end than the *umbumbuluzo*. The hides came from

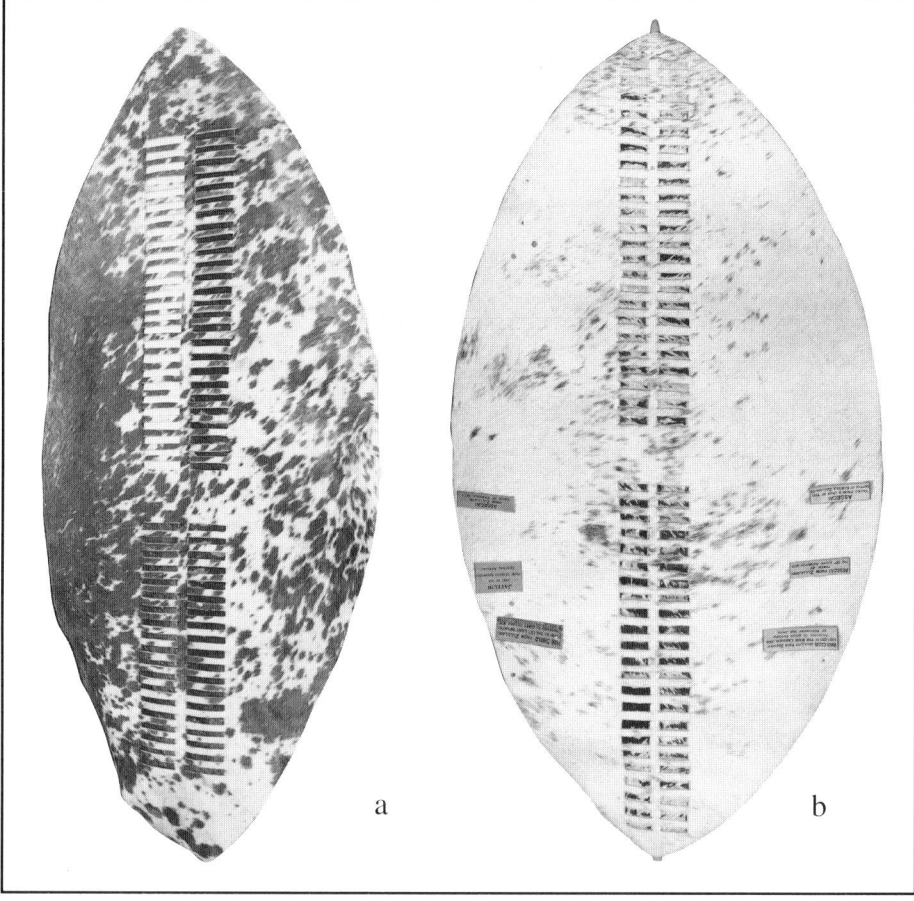

Shield terminology: the precision with which the different markings on war-shields were labelled is suggested by the different terms to describe these two similar patterns. (a) is an ihwanqa shield; its markings are more distinct than the rather more subtle mottling on (b), which was known as umpunga. (a: Africana Museum, Johannesburg; b: Osborne House Collection)

a

b

cattle in the royal herds; the nation had collective owner-ship of thousands of head of cattle, tended on their behalf by the king, and quartered at the royal homesteads around the country. These cattle were usually sorted according to the colour of their hides, and the king would grant a particular pattern of hide for a new *ibutho* to use for shields. Two shields would be cut from each hide. They were cleaned and prepared so that they were flexible enough to work with but sufficiently stiff to deflect a spear-thrust. Two rows of slits were cut down the centre, and strips of hide, known as *amagabelo*, were threaded through. These folded over on the back to secure a shield-stick, which served to stiffen the entire construction. Strips of civet fur were wound round the projecting top of the stick for decorative effect, while the bottom end of the stick was cut to a point. The shield was held by a small handle, fashioned from the *amagabelo* strips, on one side of the shield. Although producing a shield was a skilled job, there seem to have been plenty of men who could do it, and the missionary Gardiner, writing in the 1830s, records that dozens of shields were produced every day at the king's *komkhulu*, from cattle slaughtered to feed the regi-ments in residence.

In the early days of the kingdom, the differences between the shield colours of the various *amabutho* were quite precise. The Zulu language includes dozens of words referring to the different markings of a hide – the different size and shape of patches, the base colour of the shield and the spots, whether the spots were at the top, bottom or sides, whether the hairs intermingled, and so on – and in Shaka's time those shield patterns that were recorded are quite specific and distinctive. Even then, however, there would have been minor differences; with two shields coming from a single hide, the markings would seldom have been identical. In later years, this precision fell away, and one can only speculate on the reasons for this. Cer-tainly, in Shaka's time the army was smaller, and cattle were more plentiful – the most reliable estimates suggest that Shaka's army numbered about 14,000 warriors, while the country was rich in cattle taken in successful raiding. By King Cetshwayo's time, the army numbered over 30,000, and there was something of a shortage of cattle. Diseases introduced by white traders had decimated the royal herds, and many hides were being exported to Natal rather than used inside Zululand. Thus, while some regi-ments in 1879 had distinctive shields, several are mentioned as having no particular colour, and at least one was granted shields of several different colours. It seems likely that the king fixed on a particular colour when *buta*'ing a new *ibutho*, then topped it up with shields of other colours if there were insufficient to go round. There are suggestions that in a regiment where colours were mixed, some uniformity was nonetheless maintained within the i*zigaba*. Thus one division might have black shields, another brown with white spots, another speckled – even if they belonged to the same *ibutho*.

A broad approach to colour-coding remained consistent throughout the kingdom's history. Black had associations of youth and vigour, and was therefore carried by the younger regiments. White symbolised experience, and in Shaka's time white shields were carried by his favourite *amabutho*, who had already distinguished themselves in battle. When the later kings allowed their *amabutho* to marry at an earlier age, however, white came increasingly to be associated with married regiments. Dark brown shields fell broadly into the 'young' category, while red-brown shields tended to be carried by older *amabutho*.

Implicit in this system is the idea that at some point during its active life an *ibutho* would need to exchange one set of shields for another. This may have happened several times, since the practical life of a shield was probably not that long, and it is possible that each time new shields were issued, the pattern changed to include more white markings. The evidence regarding this point is inconclusive, although the missionary Gardiner witnessed an interesting ceremony at King Dingane's *komkhulu* in 1836. A regiment arrived to 'beg' new shields of the king, and their

senior *induna* was called out to give an account of their service. He was challenged by one of the king's advisors, who belittled the regiment's record, and the *induna* was required to justify his claim before the king. Dingane listened to the exchange good-humouredly, and promised to supply fresh shields if the regiment succeeded in one further expedition. The warriors greeted this judgement enthusiastically and marched away, but Gardiner formed the opinion that the proceedings were merely symbolic, since the order for fresh campaigning was countermanded. The regiment returned a few days later to claim their shields. Sadly, Gardiner gives us no clues whether the shield patterns differed in any way from those which had been previously issued, but logic suggests that they did.

The shields were kept in stores called *umyango*, dome-shaped thatched structures which were raised about eight feet off the ground on stilts. This kept the shields out of the reach of damp and, more particularly, rats and white ants, which could easily destroy them. Even when a regiment was stationed in its *ikhanda*, shields were not necessarily used on a daily basis, and the warriors seem to have drawn them when necessary, returning them to the stores at the end of each day, unless actually setting off on campaign. Gardiner mentions that when he saw the *ibutho* claim their new shields, the warriors thumped them heartily with their sticks to make sure they were sound. No doubt each man took advantage of any minor variations in size to find one that best suited his height and weight, but although there are suggestions that important men carried the same shield on different occasions, it seems unlikely that this would have been the case for ordinary warriors.

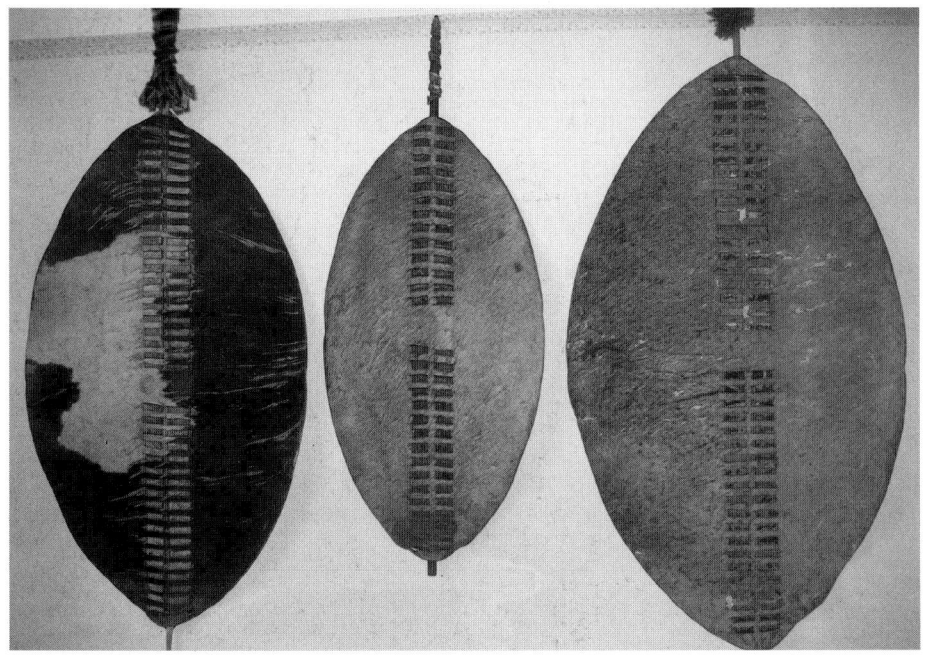

Three war-shields from the 1879 period, the smaller umbhumbhulozu *type, flanked by two* izihlangu.

WEAPONS

There is no direct contemporary evidence relating to the weapon types and fighting techniques used in the pre-Shakan era; even most Zulu stories relating to them have all the rosy glow of nostalgia for a past golden age. It was supposedly an age when fighting was conducted according to gentlemanly rules, when the main weapon was the throwing spear, and when casualties were light. All of that apparently changed when Shaka introduced a heavy-bladed stabbing spear and close-quarter fighting techniques: battles became brutal struggles for survival. To what extent this image is accurate is impossible to say, but it is true that the throwing spear is not a particularly destructive weapon, and that by the time the first whites arrived in Zululand, in 1824, the Zulus were committed to a concept of hand-to-hand fighting with stabbing weapons.

The spear

The Zulu man grew up accustomed to weapons. Although some types were specifically designed for fighting, the spear was an everyday essential in a culture which boasted no other cutting tool and where weapons were needed to slaughter beasts, to hunt, and for self-protection. There were many different types, each varying in the length of the blade and the shaft, according to its purpose. The most common type of throwing spear was the *isijula*, which had a blade about 7 in. long, with several inches of visible tang set into a narrow shaft about 3 ft long. Its effectiveness was entirely dependent on range: having grown up throwing sticks at moving targets, the average Zulu could throw a spear with considerable accuracy and velocity up to 30 yd. At that distance it could transfix a human torso, and, if caught straight on, could easily penetrate a hide shield. At longer distances its effectiveness declined noticeably: the drag of the shaft caused it to waver in flight, causing a loss of accuracy and velocity.

Innovations by Shaka

Shaka apparently ordered his warriors to discard the stabbing spear, and carry instead a heavier weapon with a broader blade and stouter haft, designed to withstand the stresses of repeated stabbing. The prototype Shakan weapon – according to legend, he called it *iklwa*, from the sucking sound it made when being pulled out – had a blade about 18 in. long and 1 ½ in. wide, with no visible tang, set into a haft about 30 in. long. The haft had a swollen end so that the hand, when wet with blood, would not slip off

A selection of typical stabbing-spear blades. One of these saw action in 1879, another in the 1906 rebellion. (SB Bourquin)

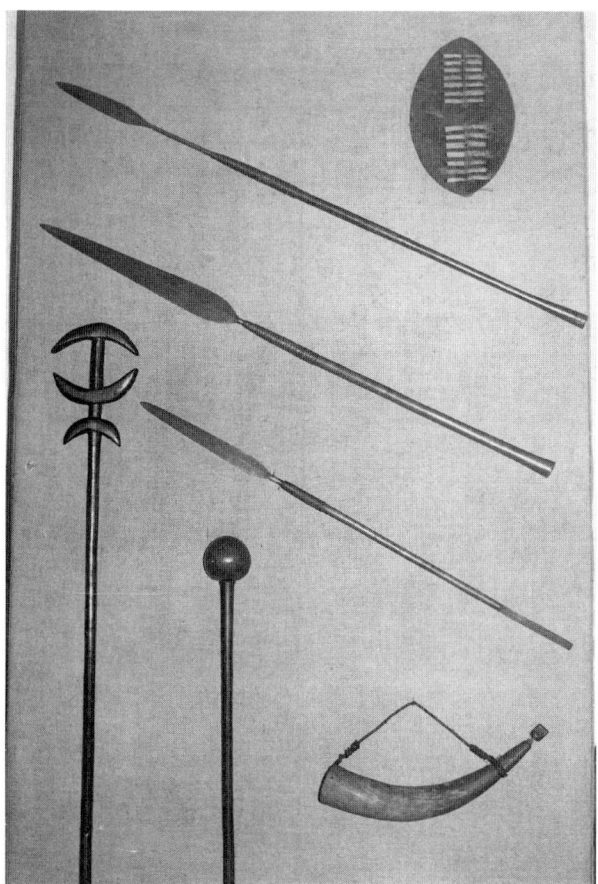

A selection of Zulu weapons. The prototype Shaka stabbing spear (centre) with a smaller variant (below) and a throwing spear (top). At the bottom are a knobkerry club and a typical powder-horn. On the left is a carved 'status stick', carried by men of rank. (Killie Campbell Africana Library)

combat, with the full weight of the body behind it. It is not clear whether this was taught to the warriors as part of their training, or whether it was merely fashionable, but the position did have a specific name –*imfukule* – and famous warriors were known to advocate its use. In the latter days of the kingdom, most stabbing weapons seem to have been smaller than the Shakan type, with blades about 14 in. long and 1 in. wide. The reason for this remains obscure: it may be that such weapons were just as effective as the heavier type, or that the trade in iron from Colonial Natal led to a decrease in the quality of the indigenous product.

Spear manufacture

The weapons were made by specialist smiths. The iron ore was collected from surface deposits, and smelted in a clay furnace heated with goatskin bellows. The ore was worked into ingots when soft, then hammered into shape and finished. The forging of iron was regarded with superstitious mistrust, and smiths tended to live on the fringes of ordinary society; it was widely rumoured that they used human fat to temper the best blades. One craftsman made the blade, and another assembled the spear, carefully selecting and cutting the hafts. A hole was bored into the end, and the tang of the blade heated and dipped into a strong vegetable glue before fitting. The join was then bound with a strip of wet bark, and sealed either with plaited cane, or with a tube of hide cut from a calf's tail. As the binding dried, it shrank, and the join became very firm. Although in combat Zulu spears occasionally burst at the join, this was very rare; it was more common for the haft to break or the blade to bend. Generally, however, the weapon was strong, sharp and more than capable of withstanding the tasks for which it was designed.

As with costume, spears were, in theory, supplied to the *amabutho* as part of the king's bounty, but again this was largely symbolic. The smiths would occasionally send a bundle of spears to the king, who then paid them in cattle. The spears were then distributed to an *ibutho* the king wished to favour. Although to receive a spear from the king was considered an honour, there were by no means enough spears to go round, and those who received them were probably *izilomo*, the king's favourite warriors. The majority of warriors would be expected to attend a muster carrying their own spears, which they apparently obtained by trading with the smiths on their own account. Spears were therefore regarded as personal property, unlike the regimental war-shields.

The club

Although almost all of traditional weapons were spears, a few warriors would have carried clubs (knobkerries) and

when withdrawing the weapon from a deep body thrust. Shaka insisted that the stabbing spear was the sole weapon carried into action, and that every warrior take good care of it; anyone returning from a fight without it was liable to accusations of cowardice.

During Dingane's reign, the throwing spear made a reappearance, perhaps in response to the first encounters with whites armed with firearms. Although the throwing spear's range was strictly limited, it at least gave the Zulus a chance to respond when fighting an enemy whose smoothbore muskets were only effective at less than 100 yards' range. By 1879 it was common for warriors to take two or three throwing spears and a stabbing spear into action; the spare spears were carried behind the shield, and a warrior would charge down on his enemy, throwing his *izijula*, then closing in with the stabbing weapon.

The stabbing spear was generally used under-arm in

Zulu blacksmiths at work. The smith (right) heats the furnace using goat-skin bellows, while his assistants beat the ore into shape.

axes. Most clubs were cut from a single piece of wood, and had a straight shaft and a round bulbous end. They were beautifully worked with a deep patina, but their use was simple enough – they were intended to beat the enemy's brain out. Axes, on the other hand, were largely ceremonial, although there are suggestions that they were sometimes carried into battle. Half-moon axes, with a tang projecting from the back of the blade, which was then sunk onto a wooden handle, were common throughout southern Africa, but the true Zulu axe, although similar, had a blade that was rather wider and longer at the top, projecting for several inches above the end of the handle. In battle the axe could be used both for chopping, and for hooking over the edge of the opponent's shield, to drag it aside.

FIREARMS

The Zulus first encountered firearms when the first Europeans arrived in the country, during King Shaka's reign. Although they caused some initial confusion, the Zulus quickly recovered, so that by the time of the first conflict with the whites – Dingane's war on the Voortrekkers, in 1838 – the Zulu army was quite prepared to face them. White traders recorded several conversations with King Shaka on the subject, and Shaka, although impressed, remained convinced that his warriors would overcome troops armed with firearms so long as they were prepared to withstand the heavy casualties they would sustain

before they could close hand-to-hand. Ironically, his view was to be put to the test in exactly those terms in 1879.

Although Shaka pressed white traders into his army, adding a small group of musketeers to his otherwise conventional forces, it was not until Dingane's reign that the Zulu made the first attempts to secure firearms. They were not very successful, and the numbers of guns involved were small. They increased, however, during Mpande's reign, when trade burgeoned between Zululand and the emerging colony of Natal. Mpande was quick to realise that a monopoly over the gun trade increased his security, against both outside aggression and internal dissent, in a very practical way. Nevertheless, the gun trade remained illegal in Natal, and the numbers of guns smuggled in remained small. (Larger numbers were probably imported through Mozambique, in the north, but even so, firearms played very little part in the civil war of 1856.)

Large-scale importation of guns into Zululand probably dates from the 1860s, when the trader John Dunn befriended the heir apparent, Prince Cetshwayo, and secured permission from Natal to supply him with arms, on the grounds that by strengthening the heir, the risk of further conflict was reduced. Throughout the 1860s and 1870s there was, in any case, a glut of guns on the world market, as technological advances in Europe and America meant that obsolete flintlock and percussion guns were dumped cheaply in the colonies. Thousands of guns were shipped in through Mozambique, many of them destined for the Zulu trade. In the 1870s an Enfield rifle, standard issue in the British Army only a dozen years before, could be bought in Zululand for as little as the cost of a sheep. Zulus recall that Dunn used to transport guns to King Cetshwayo's *komkhulu* by the wagon-load. Although Cetshwayo tried to maintain the monopoly of trade, distributing guns among his *amabutho* as a mark of royal patronage, inevitably many of the regional *izikhulu* traded on their own account, thereby increasing their own power and influence. Estimates of the number of guns inside Zululand before the start of the Anglo-Zulu war vary considerably, but they certainly numbered thousands, and most warriors had access to some sort of firearm.

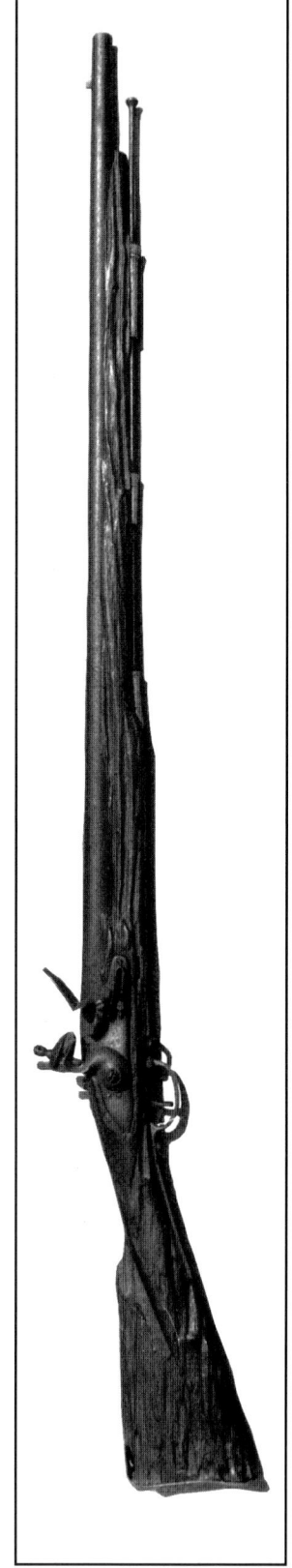

British Tower-mark Brown Bess musket, used by the Zulus in the war of 1879. The wood has been heavily damaged by termites. (Zulu Cultural Museum, oNdini)

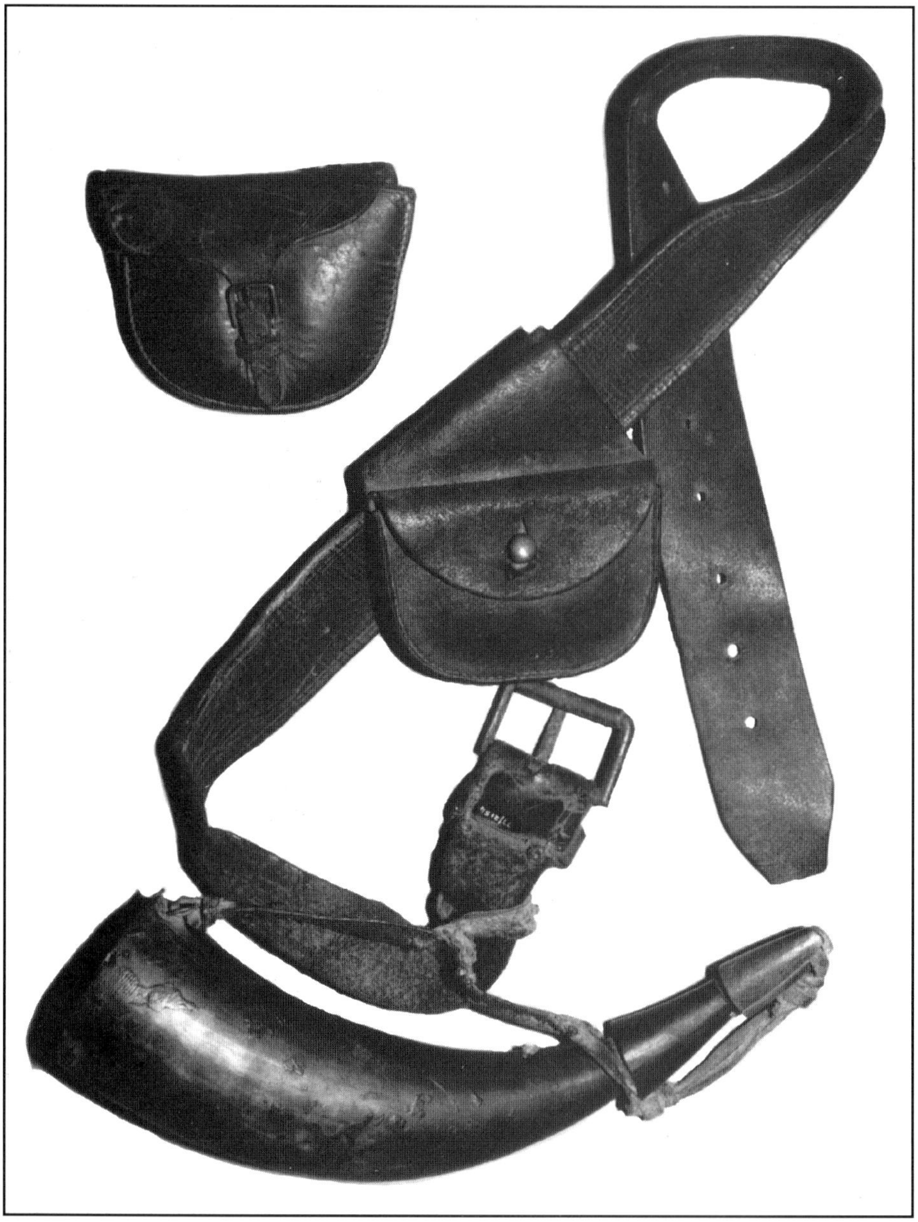

Below: A powder horn and belt taken from the body of a Zulu killed at the battle of oNdini. It is typical of the improvised contraptions the Zulus were forced to adopt to carry their ammunition. (Local History Museum, Durban)

Deficiencies in weaponry

If the quantity was sufficient, however, the quality certainly was not. The type of gun found in Zululand in the greatest number was probably the old Brown Bess – the British military issue musket of the Napoleonic Wars, bearing the Tower mark. By the 1870s these guns were 50 years out of date, and many were in poor condition. European and American guns of various makes were also common, and there were also large numbers of percussion rifles, and a smattering of good-quality hunting pieces. Although a handful of Zulus could shoot well, probably trained by the white hunters who operated in the country in considerable numbers in the 1850s and 1860s, most had only the vaguest concept of the principles of musketry. Guns were seldom cleaned, and became rusty; many had never been accurate except at short range when they were new, and most Zulus believed that the higher the sights were set, the further a gun would shoot. At the beginning of the 1879 war, the king was aware of some of these deficiencies, and called up several of the *amabutho* to practise musket drill, but with few enough experts to advise them, the results were disappointing.

Zulu fire in battle was, therefore, heavy but inaccurate, and accuracy was further compromised by poor-quality powder and improvised ammunition. Good-quality shot was hard to come by, and the Zulu were forced to rely on home-made projectiles, ranging from stones dipped in lead to pieces of iron, broken from cooking pots and hammered roughly into shape. Powder was carried in horns, which may have been traded from Natal, and shot in all manner of ways, including leather belts bought from traders. After the battle of Gingindlovu, the British found Zulu dead whose pouches were full of British newspapers, letters and documents which had been looted from the field of Isandlwana and were being used as wadding. Indeed, over 1,000 British Martini-Henry rifles, together with assorted carbines and revolvers, and 50,000 rounds of ammunition were captured at Isandlwana. Although the king demanded that these weapons be brought before him, he pragmatically allowed each warrior who had taken one to keep it. The distribution of so many modern firearms did lead to rather better results at battles later in the war, but Zulu firepower remained disappointing. Those warriors who had not secured a Martini-Henry resorted to biting out the bullets from looted British cartridges and using the powder in their old muzzle-loaders.

An inhlenla, *a staff with a barbed blade, carried only by men of the highest rank. This example is said to have belonged to Prince*

Dabulamanzi kaMpande, who led the attack on Rorke's Drift. (Natal Museum)

ON CAMPAIGN

Preparations

The Zulu army could be mobilised within a matter of days. The decision to undertake a campaign was made by the king, in discussion with his *ibandla* council, and the word would then be sent out to the *izinduna* commanding the district *amakhanda*. All messages were carried by runners, who could cover great distances every day at an economical jogging pace. The district officers were expected to know their areas well enough to summon the fighting men as quickly as possible. This was often done by word of mouth, shouting from one hill-top homestead to another. When he received the news that the army was summoned, a warrior would make his way as quickly as possible to his regimental *ikhanda*, taking with him his weapons, and accompanied, if possible, by a young brother or son to carry for him.

In the early days of the kingdom, there are suggestions that the *amabutho* mustered for war wearing their full ceremonial regalia; certainly the white adventurer Fynn saw one of Shaka's expeditions setting off fully panoplied. It is not clear whether this was worn into action – it may have been packed away in the sleeping mats once the

amabutho had departed from the king – but it does seem likely that more regalia was retained in the 1820s than was the case in 1879. On the eve of the Anglo-Zulu war, King Cetshwayo apparently ordered his men to assemble without regalia and 'ready for fighting'. In the subsequent battles, the British noted that very little regalia was worn into action, although there were some exceptions. Generally, it seems that a number of factors influenced the choice of what was retained and what was left at home: older, more conservative *amabutho* seem to have worn more than younger men; and warriors who lived near the scene of the fighting seem to have worn more than those who had to march a long way. Certainly the more fragile and expensive items were generally left at home, and some pieces, such as the heavy cow-tail necklaces, were in any case uncomfortable to wear for long periods. Lighter regalia such as head-bands, perhaps with a few distinctive feathers, and cow-tail leg- and arm-ornaments were more likely to be retained, but there was considerable variation, even within a single *ibutho*. *Izinduna* may well have retained the parts which indicated their status, but most warriors probably fought wearing nothing but *umutsha* loin-coverings and a necklace with charms and medicines to ward off evil.

Those warriors who lived nearest the king reported straight to the *komkhulu*, where they were sorted into their *amabutho* by the king's attendants. Those whose *ikhanda* was in the vicinity were directed to occupy it, and the remainder were appointed sheltered spots nearby to erect temporary shelters and wait for the rest of their regiment. Those in the outlying districts reported to their regimental *amakhanda*, where they were assembled by their own officers, issued shields, and then marched to the king. It was expected that the entire army should assemble within three or four days, and woe betide any *ibutho* that was late without reason. *Izinduna* might be deprived of their command and fined, and the men themselves set upon and beaten by their colleagues in other regiments.

Pre-campaign rituals

When the army was assembled, it was crucial that it should undergo a preparatory 'doctoring' ritual before embarking on the campaign. The imminence of violent conflict meant that the dark supernatural forces, *umnyama* – literally 'blackness' – of which the Zulus lived in constant dread, were particularly close to the surface of daily life. Important measures had to be taken to prevent the nation from

A recent study of a Zulu in traditional dress, showing the head-band. Note the ways artificial 'tails', tied to the back of the head-dress, have been arranged to hang decoratively at the front. Lighter items such as these were often retained in action.

falling victim to any ascendancy by psychic means (*ithonya*) practised by the enemy and to prevent the king and his warriors from being ritually polluted. The entire army was marched to a selected spot where *izinyanga* – the doctors who looked after the welfare of the nation – had dug deep, narrow pits in the ground. The warriors were summoned in small groups and required to drink a specially prepared liquid from pots; this was *muthi*, medicine designed to cleanse them and prepare them for the ceremonies needed to make them ready for war. They were then required to regurgitate the liquid into the hole; although the *muthi* contained a strong emetic, it was still necessary for some warriors to induce vomiting by sticking their fingers down their throat. This process took some time, and as they finished, the warriors retired to a nearby hillside to recover. The ceremony was the first step in a process designed to bind the army together, and when it was over, the *izinyanga* collected a small sample of vomit – which

Left: Zulu weapons and artefacts. An isihlangu shield, flanked by throwing and stabbing spears (left) and chiefs' sticks (right). In the foreground are a number of knob-kerries, gourds, spoons and wooden head-rests.

represented the very essence of the nation under arms – on a twist of grass, then carefully filled in the hole to prevent outsiders from discovering it. The grass was added to the *inkatha yezwe ya'kwaZulu*, the 'coil of the nation', a grass rope bound in python skin which was an immensely powerful symbol of the unity of the kingdom.

After the vomiting ceremony, the army was marched back to the great place. Here the king, who had himself been smeared with medicines to allow him to commune with the ancestral spirits, received them. It was now necessary for an appointed *ibutho* – often the youngest, so that over the years each regiment took its turn – to kill a

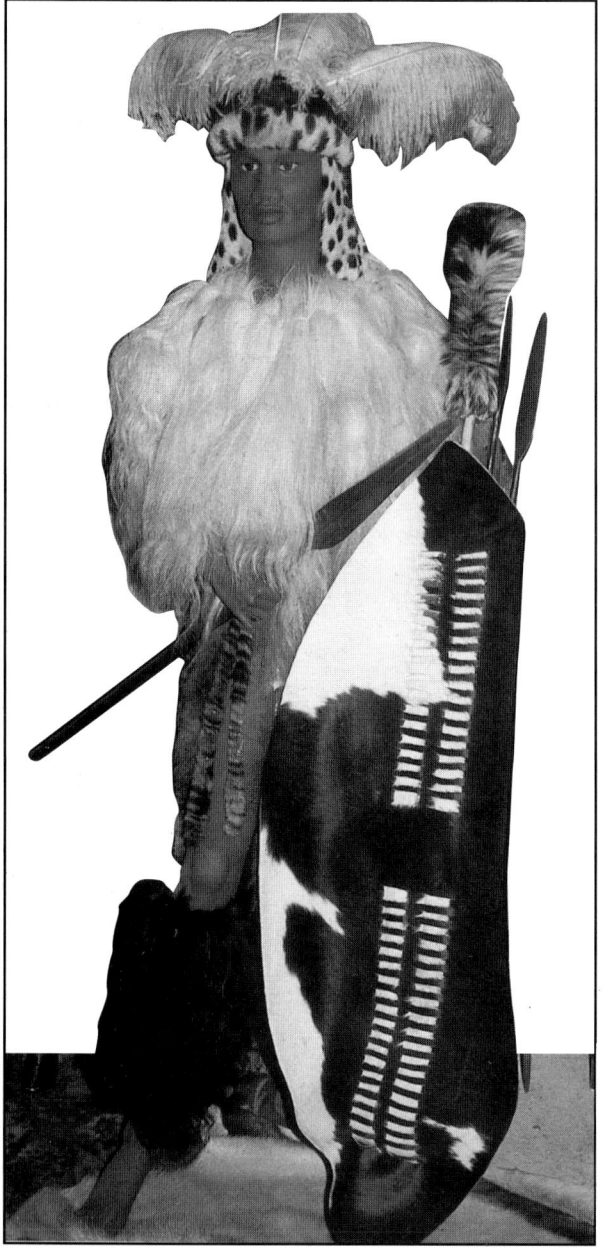

A magnificent recreation of the full splendour of the warriors' ceremonial regalia. Note the cow-tail 'necklace', head-band and ear-flaps, and the variety of feathers in the head-dress. (Blockhouse Museum, Ladysmith)

black bull with their bare hands. The bull had been selected for its fierceness, since this ceremony represented the nation's strength and ability to overcome its enemies, and a placid bull would undermine the symbolism. It was not unusual for several men to be gored or trampled before the bull was wrestled to the ground and its neck broken. It was then cut up by the *izinyanga*, who roasted the meat on bonfires of willow-wood, and carefully destroyed every remaining particle of the carcass, to prevent it being stolen for *muthi* by the enemy. When the meat was cooked, it was cut into long strips, *umbengo*, and sprinkled with medicines. The army was then assembled in a circle in the central enclosure of the *komkhulu*, and the strips of meat tossed among them. Each warrior was supposed to grab a strip, bite off a piece, and throw the strip back into the crowd. He was not supposed to swallow the meat, but in the excitement of the moment, that often occurred, especially if food had been in short supply since the army had mustered. The excitement was intense, and on a hot day it was not unknown for warriors to faint, and be helped out of the press of bodies by friends and colleagues.

Spiritual preparations

The doctoring ceremonies took several days to complete, and while they were going on, the king would summon two or three pairs of *amabutho* before him. These regiments were *uphalane* – they followed closely upon each other in age, were considered linked in some way, and were often called out to serve together. The king called upon them to say what they intended to do in the coming fight, and the *amabutho* challenged one another. Individual warriors would stand out and *giya*, performing the solitary display of dancing and shadow-fighting which represented their past victories, and call out to individuals known to them in the rival regiment. 'So-and-so, son of so-and-so', they would shout, 'if I don't kill more of the enemy than you, you may take my sister, my cattle, or my homestead.' The challenged man was honour-bound to respond, and any failure to do so was looked upon as a sign of cowardice. In fact, however, the wagers were purely notional, and served to stoke up the rivalries between the regiments; although the challenges were recalled after the campaign, no property ever changed hands. In 1879 King Cetshwayo first set the iNgobamakhosi against the uKhandempemvu, and then the uMbonambi against the uNokhenke, and it is no coincidence that these regiments played a conspicuous part in the subsequent fighting.

When the main ceremonies were complete, the *amabutho* were once again assembled in a circle. It was now time for the king to address them, to explain the reasons for the coming campaign, and to give them advice. King Shaka led many of his campaigns in person, though he was the only king to do so; in 1879 King Cetshwayo apparently explained to the army that he had no idea why the British were attacking him. 'I have not gone over the seas to look for the white man', he is supposed to have said, 'yet they have come into my country . . . They want to take me. What shall I do?' The army, of course, responded indignantly, 'Give the matter to us! . . . They shall not going to take you while we are here!' Henry Fynn left an account of Shaka's army setting off on campaign with what was probably typical instructions:

'A speech was made by Mbikwana in which he showed what the aggravating cause was that called for revenge, namely, the attempt on the life of the King. The order to march was given, and they were directed to spare neither man, woman, child nor dog. They were to burn their huts, to break the stones on which their corn was ground, and so prove their attachment to their king.'

Before the army departed, however, there was one final administration of medicines. This time the *izinyanga* spattered each warrior front and back with a liquid which may have included items of spiritual power stolen from the enemy. This ensured that the departing army would be safe from the enemy's weapons, and would overcome them. Sometimes, if the *izinyanga* had managed to obtain one of the enemy's weapons, the warriors would be required to file past, chanting appropriate incantations, so that the enemy's weapons would all be blunted. In 1879 those warriors who had firearms held them muzzle-down over medicines that were smouldering on a pot-sherd. The

Demonstrating the effectiveness of the throwing spear. At a range of 20 yards the spear easily struck – and penetrated – the shields set up as a target. At this distance – about 30 yards – it was a good deal less accurate and effective.

smoke rising up the barrel ensured that their own guns would fire straight. To counter the enemy's weapons, medicines were smeared on each man's forehead, to make him invulnerable to British bullets.

When the ceremonies were complete, the warriors had entered a psychological state in which they were fit only for war. The ceremonies had prepared their spirits to suffer the consequences of killing others or being killed themselves; they were set apart from the normal round of civilian life, and could not be returned to it until they had undergone the counterpart cleansing ceremonies at the end of the campaign. They were required to abstain from most of the practices of daily life, and to avoid the company of their women-folk at all costs. Zulu warfare was usually short, and even on a major campaign it was unusual for the army to be away for more than a few months. The reasons for this were both practical and spiritual: it was difficult for the warriors to maintain this psychological state indefinitely, and as time went on their absence from their civilian roles would be increasingly felt. It was not merely for strategic reasons, therefore, that the Zulus' military outlook was aggressive, and shaped by the need to close with the enemy and force a decisive clash as quickly as possible.

On The March

As the *amabutho* set out on a campaign, the regiments sang various chants and shouted war-cries. Each regiment had its own cry, which usually recalled some past glory, although during combat it was more usual to use the national cry. The order of march was dictated by the king, and it was considered a great honour to be the regiment appointed to the vanguard. On setting off, the army marched for the first day or two in a single column. As they drew nearer the enemy, they split into two columns, so that one was always ready to support the other if they were attacked by surprise. The advance was screened by a complex system of spies and scouts, who served not only to provide intelligence of the enemy's movements, but also to mask their own by keeping back the enemy's scouts. It was unusual for the Zulus to embark on a campaign without first having sent spies to scout out a viable route, and in 1879 the army was fighting on its home ground, so that no matter where in the country it was operating, there were usually men present who knew the terrain well. Spies were expected, if possible, to infiltrate the enemy's camps and secure as much information about their intentions and dispositions as possible. In 1879 the British were haunted by the possibility that their black auxiliaries, wagon-drivers and cooks were infiltrated by Zulus, and it is quite possible that they were. Behind the spies came large bodies of scouts, who were, in effect, skirmishers. Two or three men known to be particularly brave and daring were picked out from each *iviyo* in the army, so that the scouts themselves numbered several companies. They were pushed out some miles ahead of the army, and were expected to deceive the enemy by passing themselves off as the main body, and attacking any enemy parties they came across. Runners constantly carried information of any developments back to the principal commanders.

Traditional fighting techniques included a combined movement of the shield, to knock the enemy off-guard, and an under-arm thrust of the stabbing spear.

Ceremonial dress

A

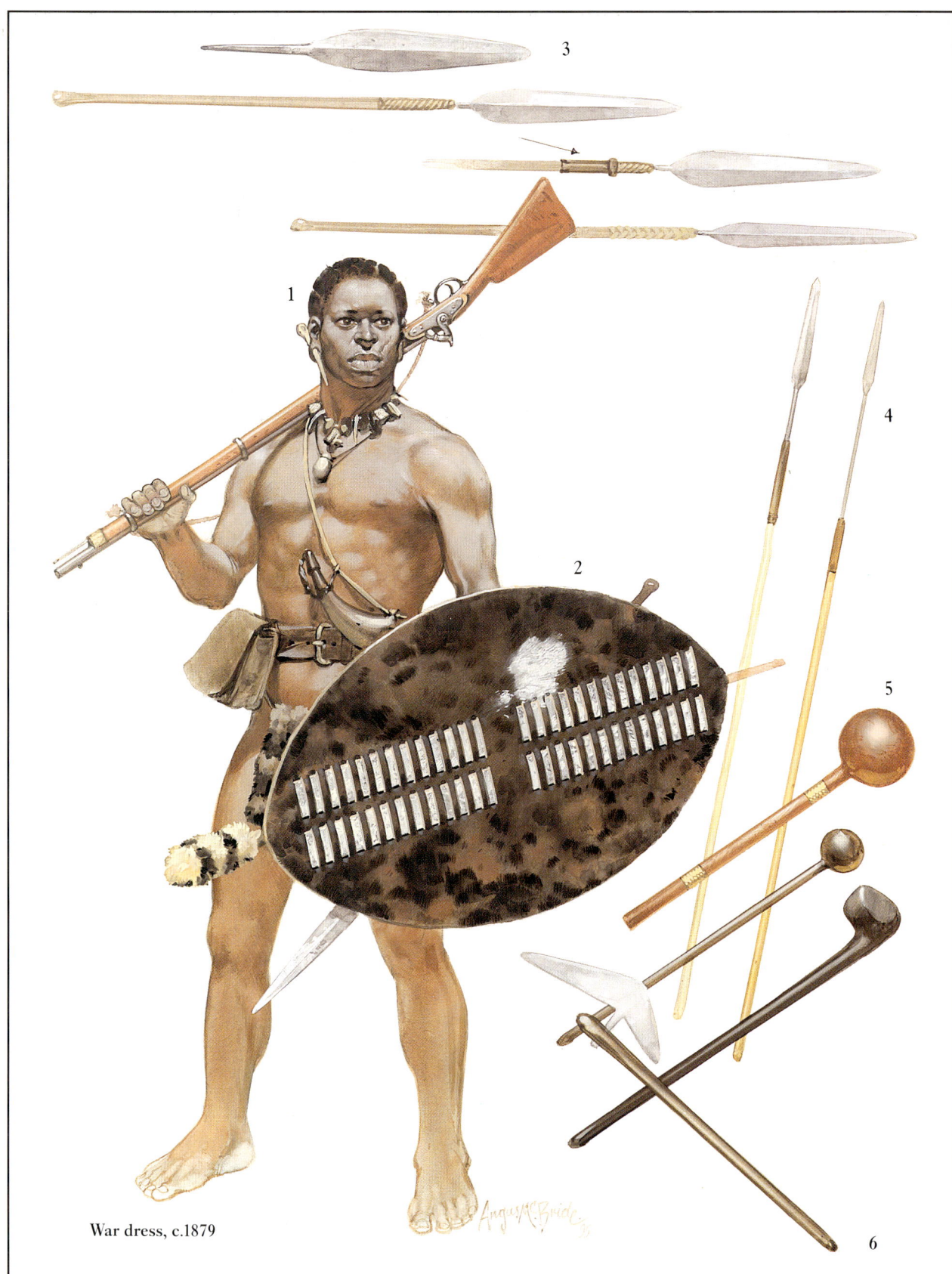

War dress, c.1879

B

a

1

b

c

2

5

6

3

4

Zulu regalia

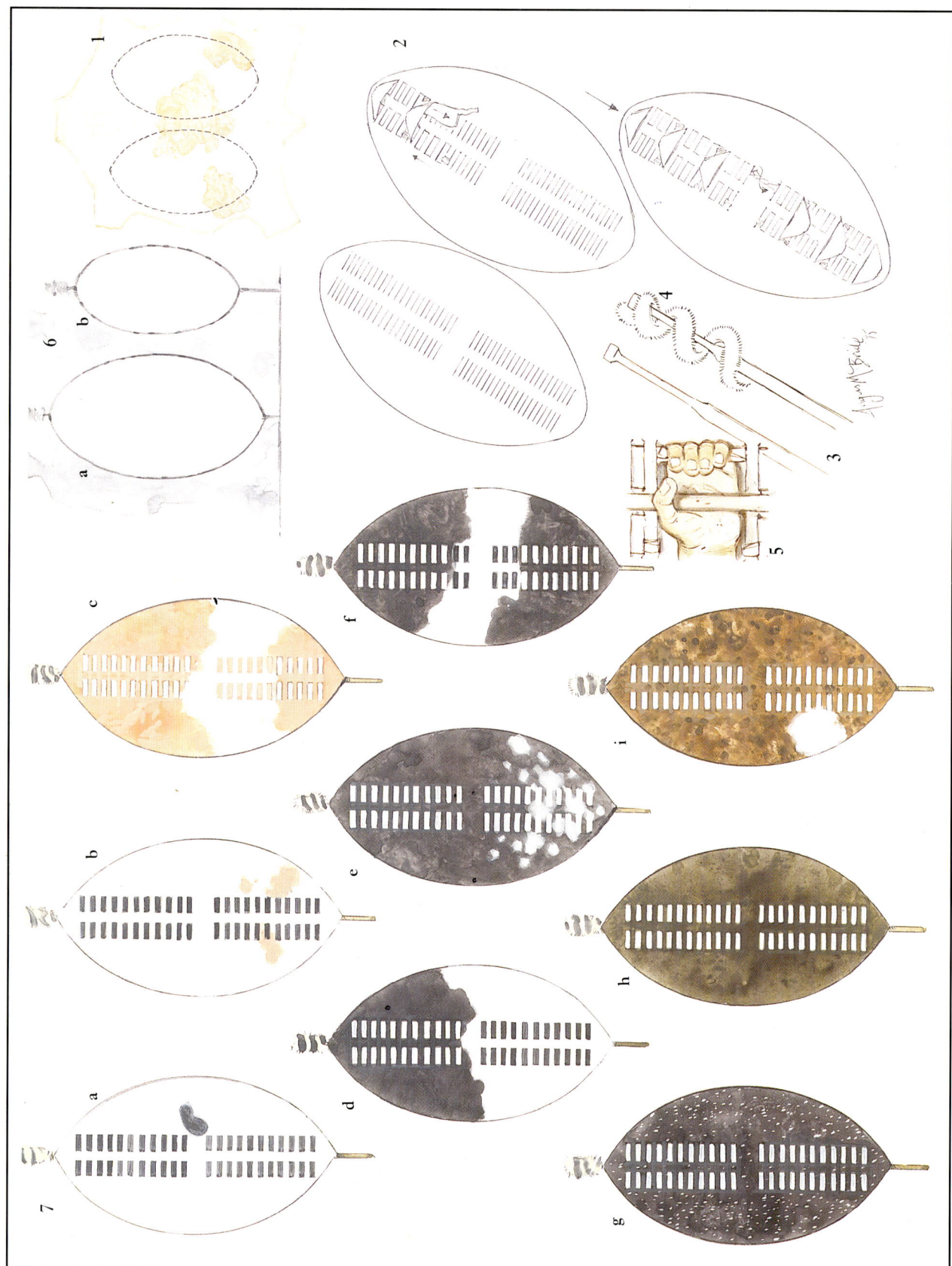

D

Cadet training

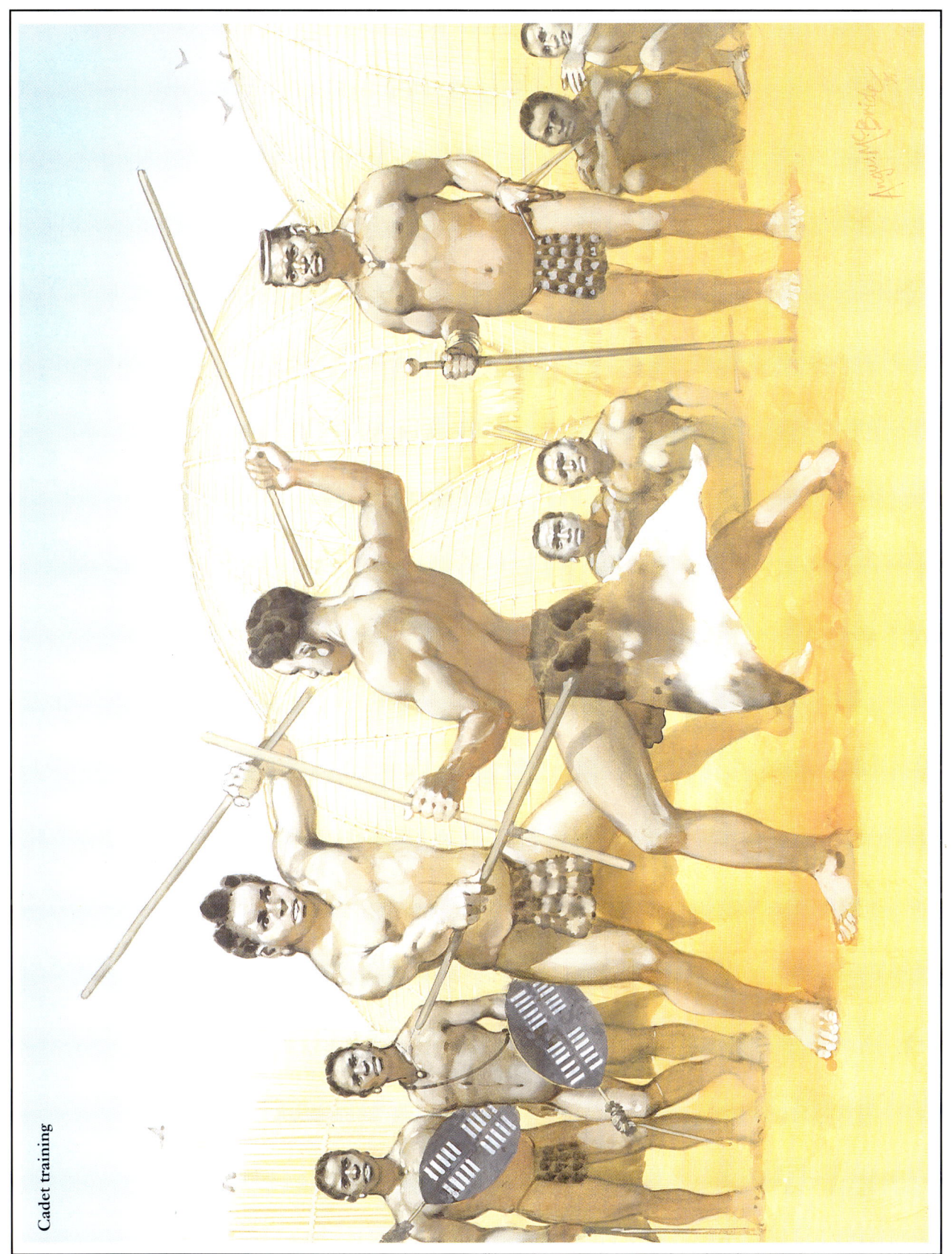

On the march, c.1879

F

G

The 'beast's horns'

H

Aftermath of Isandlwana, 1879

J

Purification from the blood of battle

L

Mobility and supply

Although the image of the Zulu army which could 'run fifty miles and fight a battle at the end of it' is largely a myth, the *amabutho* were certainly highly mobile. The army was, in effect, a collection of individuals who were used to walking for long periods across country, and it is interesting to note that in 1879 the army averaged between 20 and 30 miles a day, keeping up this pace for days at a stretch. Having no baggage with them beyond what they could carry, they were able to negotiate natural obstacles that would have confounded European armies, scaling steep hills and rocky slopes, and forging rivers by forming a human chain. On a long march, the men would remove the sticks from their shields and carry the hide rolled up.

Food was something of a problem. Most warriors probably set off on campaign with a handful of rations carried in a skin bag – a calf's liver and a handful of roasted mealies were most popular – and for the first few days the army would be accompanied by the *izindibi*, and perhaps some of the warriors' sisters, carrying food. These non-combatants marched on the flanks of the army, towards the rear, and out of harm's way, but they gradually dwindled away as the provisions they carried were consumed. In Shaka's time these were usually sufficient to get the army beyond Zululand's borders, but in 1879 all of the campaigning actually took place on Zulu soil. Since it was customary, after the first few days, for the army to live by foraging, this presented problems; many Zulu civilians abandoned their homesteads as the war approached and retired to places of refuge, and their grain-pits and any livestock they had abandoned were at the mercy of the passing Zulu army. Although the evidence suggests that the *izinduna* tried to keep their men under control as much as possible, the passage of the army could still be devastating. Cattle were rounded up, driven along 'on the hoof', and only slaughtered for consumption. In 1879 there are suggestions that the warriors in the field were running short of food, and in any case the Zulu habit of eating mid-morning meant that they went hungry into any battles which started before then. In some unsuccessful campaigns – notably Shaka's disastrous Balule campaign of 1828 – witnesses record the spectacle of the army trickling back home, a succession of emaciated and half-starving individuals whose spirit had been badly undermined by hunger.

At the end of each day's march, the *izinduna* would appoint a place to bivouac, and select sentries from among the ranks. If there was time, and the enemy were not too near, the men were allowed to build temporary shelters by cutting branches, tying them into a rough framework, then

A recent photo of a Zulu in traditional dress, wearing a leopardskin head-band and cow-tails – probably the most complex items to be retained in battle in the 19th century. The foam padding around the handle suggests just how hard on the knuckles the shield can be.

piling grass over the top. Fires were lit and food cooked. The British, examining one such bivouac after the battle of Gingindlovu, found the hillsides around 'seamed' by paths in the grass, marking the army's approach, and the camp-site littered with abandoned sleeping mats and other debris. If the enemy were close, however, and if wood was in short supply, as when the main army encamped in the Ngwebeni valley before Isandlwana, no fires were allowed and no shelters were built. The warriors had to get what sleep they could, on mats if they had them, or the ground.

EXPERIENCE OF BATTLE

The Zulu military outlook was essentially aggressive. Partly this was moulded by the practical needs of a citizen army to avoid prolonged campaigning, and partly it was the result of the precedent set by King Shaka, whose attitude – as far as one can tell – was always to attack the enemy as swiftly and as heavily as possible. Defensive battles were rare: conflict usually consisted of a rapid attack in the open. Night attacks were avoided – it was a time of *umnyama*, and difficult in any case to co-ordinate troop movements, but dawn was a favourite time. Where possible the Zulu would attack 'in the horns of the morning', in the first grey light when the horns of cattle stood out against the brightening sky. At such a time the enemy might be caught off-guard, and at a psychologically low ebb.

Before an attack was launched, the army would be formed into a final *umkhumbi*, and a last sprinkling of

Prince Gideon Zulu leading the amabutho *in a modern ceremony. He is wearing the traditional costume of a man of the highest rank: a collar of leopardskin, a magnificent* insimba *kilt, and crane feathers in his head-dress.*

medicines administered by the *izinyanga*. The senior *izinduna* would make a final address, reminding the warriors of their duty to the king, recalling their past glories, and urging them not to disgrace the spirits of the ancestors. At Isandlwana the army had not been expecting to attack on 22 January because it was the day before the new moon – a time of *umnyama*. When it was discovered by British patrols, the attack developed spontaneously, and afterwards many Zulus attributed the losses they had suffered to the fact that they had not been fully doctored. Before the battle of Khambula, Chief Mnyamana Buthelezi, the king's senior advisor and the most powerful *isikhulu* in the kingdom, addressed the warriors, but stressed the consequences of defeat so much that the warriors were unsettled.

Isandlwana

The battle of Isandlwana, on 22 January 1879, was, paradoxically, the Zulu army's finest hour, and its death-knell. It demonstrated that the army's strengths could work to devastating advantage, even against an enemy armed with an infinitely superior weapon technology. Yet the losses sustained by the Zulus revealed the grim underlying truth, that the army was painfully vulnerable to concentrated firepower, and by their victory at Isandlwana, the Zulus merely provoked a merciless British backlash, which did not let up until their capacity to resist had been broken.

In 1879 King Cetshwayo had perhaps 30,000 men available to fight in the field, with a small reserve of middle-aged men kept back at oNdini to guard his person. The great army mustered in the third week of January and underwent the necessary rituals, before being sent to attack the invading British columns. Some of them were directed to reinforce the local forces defending the coastal sector, but most of them were sent to 'eat up' the British Centre Column, which had crossed into Zululand at Rorke's Drift. This army was over 20,000 strong, and consisted of almost all of the nation's best fighting material; the uKhandempemvu, iNgobamakhosi, uVe, iSangqu, uMbonambi, uNokheke, uDududu, iMbube, uThulwana, iNdlondlo, uDloko and iNdluyengwe *amabutho* were present in strength, along with a few companies from the uMxapho and other regiments fighting on the coast. At the king's insistence, the army marched slowly to the front, and on the 21st took up a position in the sheltered Ngwebeni valley, five miles from a distinctive rocky outcrop known as Isandlwana, where

A group of warriors in the abbreviated ceremonial costume which constituted 'war-dress'. (Killie Campbell Africana Library)

the British had established a camp the day before. Although the Zulu had moved directly across the front of the British line of advance, their scouts had effectively kept British patrols at bay and their presence so near to the camp was unsuspected. Indeed that night a foray from the camp discovered Zulu elements moving in the army's wake, an encounter which so misled the British commander Lord Chelmsford, that before dawn on the 22nd he took nearly half his force out of Isandlwana to search for the impi in hills about twelve miles away from their true location. The Zulu had no intention of fighting on the 22nd, but shortly before noon a patrol from the camp gave chase to a party of Zulu foragers, and stumbled on the concealed army. An unknown warrior of the uNokhenke described the initial encounter:

'. . . *a small herd of cattle came past our line from our right, being driven down by some of our scouts, and just when they were opposite to the [uKhandempemvu] regiment, a body of mounted men, on the hill to the west, were seen galloping, evidently trying to cut them off. When several hundred yards off, they perceived the [uKhandempemvu], and, dismounting, fired a volley at them and then retired. The [uKhandempemvu] at once jumped up and charged . . .'*

The nearby *amabutho*, seeing the uKhandempemvu rush forward, streamed out of the valley after them. The attack therefore began spontaneously, without any last-minute doctoring or guidance of the senior *izinduna*. Nevertheless, by the time the regiments had covered the three or four miles necessary to bring them within sight of the camp, the regimental commanders had formed them into the 'chest and horns' formation. The attack caught the British unprepared, with the British commander deploying his forces piecemeal, unaware of both the direction and true extent of the Zulu attack. The Zulus were exposed to heavy fire, particularly as they crested a line of hills above the camp, and for a while the chest and left horn stalled. According to uMhoti, a warrior of the uKhandempemvu:

'*when the soldiers who lay on the flat in front of the camp poured volley, after volley, into the impi we crouched down and dared not advance a step.'*

Yet the British line was over-extended. The regular infantry, who formed the backbone of the defence, were spread in extended order over a wide area, whilst the right flank was secured by mounted troops who, having taken up a secure position in a donga, were unable to hold back the Zulu left. Running low on ammunition the mounted men abandoned the donga and fell back on the camp. With their flank wide open, the infantry also ceased firing. UMhoti gave a graphic account of what happened next:

'Then, at the sound of a bugle the firing ceased at a breath, and the whole British force rose from the ground and retired on the tents. Like a flame the whole Zulu army sprang to its feet and darted upon them and a hand-to-hand conflict ensued amongst the tents, the main body of soldiers fighting and retiring towards the neck.'

By the time the British had reached the camp, not only had the Zulus in front of them charged home, but the Zulu right, having swung round behind Isandlwana largely unseen, had cut off the line of retreat and was threatening their rear. The fighting raged hand-to-hand; years later Sofikasho Zungu of the uVe's most vivid impression of the battle was of 'a twisting mass of soldiers and natives fighting' amidst a confusion of noise, smoke and dust. Mehlokazulu kaSihayo, a junior *induna* in the iNgobama-khosi, described the last stages of the battle:

'The resistance was stout . . . it took a long time to drive back the English forces there; they killed us and we killed them, and the fight was kept up for a long time. The British troops became helpless, because they had no ammunition, and the Zulus killed them.'

The Zulu encirclement of Isandlwana had been almost completely successful, and it was due solely to stands such as these that any British troops managed to slip through the cordon and escape. Of 1,700 British and Natal African troops in the camp at the start of the battle, 1,300 were killed, including nearly 700 British infantry. It was a victory of startling proportions, and the British were temporarily thrown onto the defensive. The successful army looted the camp, carrying away hundreds of modern Martini-Henry rifles, ammunition, and the choicest items from among the wagon-loads of supplies the British had brought with them. Yet as many as a thousand Zulus were killed outright in the battle, and perhaps as many again were wounded. Indeed there were so many men injured that the army lingered in the vicinity of the battlefield for several days, waiting for them to recover sufficiently to travel, or die. More ominously in the aftermath of Isandlwana, the uThulwana, iNdlondlo, uDloko and iNdluyengwe *amabutho* went on to attack the defended border post at Rorke's Drift, and despite the fact that they outnumbered the British garrison 40:1, were driven off with heavy casualties after ten hours fighting. The lesson was not lost on the British; it was Rorke's Drift, rather

Warriors skirmishing outside Eshowe in 1879. Note the way the artist has shown them making good use of cover, and carrying firearms and traditional weapons. Supports rush up in open file from the rear; in the foreground is a temporary grass shelter, typical of those constructed as encampments on campaign.

The face of battle: for the Zulu, combat consisted of a short, violent struggle at hand-to-hand. Paul Jamin's painting of the death of the Prince Imperial, 1879. (Reunion des Musées Nationaux)

than Isandlwana, which would set the pattern for future battles in the Anglo-Zulu war, and ultimately spell the destruction of not only the army, but the kingdom itself.

Battle tactics

There was no great distinction between the tactics used for minor skirmishes and those for major set-piece battles. Wherever possible the Zulus attacked in a formation known as the *impondo zankomo*, the 'beast's horns'. This consisted of four tactical units: the *izimpondo* or horns which rushed out to surround the enemy, and the *isifuba* or chest which mounted a frontal assault. If circumstances allowed, one horn would make use of natural cover to try to conceal its approach, to deceive the enemy as to its intentions. A reserve, the *umuva* or loins, was held back and used to plug any gap which might develop in the attack. The attack was carried out at a pace described by British observers as 'a very fast half-walk, half-run', probably the equivalent of a jogging pace, and making good use of cover. Indeed, the British were astonished in 1879 to see the speed and efficiency of the Zulu attack, noting the way that long columns deployed into open ranks, with knots of evenly spaced warriors running forward from cover to cover. As the 'chest and horns' closed in, the formations inevitably became tighter, but it was only when the warriors were within 200–300 yds that they broke into a fast run, and presented a solid body.

If the army was fighting en masse, it was usual for the younger, unmarried *amabutho* to make up the encircling horns, trading their speed for the experience of the more senior men, who composed the chest. These dispositions were apparently made by the senior *izinduna*, but the whole tactic was so deeply ingrained in the Zulu outlook that the individual warriors took up their positions instinctively. At Isandlwana there was no time to make formal dispositions, but by the time the Zulu army came within sight of the British camp, the regimental commanders had pushed the *amabutho* into line. Commands were carried by messengers and communicated by shouts or whistles, and it was unusual for warriors to hang back in the face of the enemy. If they did, as at Isandlwana, when the British fire was too heavy to allow them to advance, they could be spurred on by war-cries or by references to the challenges they had issued to one another before the campaign. At Isandlwana, the uKhandempemvu were urged on by an *induna* who reminded them that King Cetshwayo 'did not order them to lie down', and the sight of the uKhandempemvu advancing led to one *induna* of the rival iNgobamakhosi to berate his men with the cry 'Why are you lying down? What was it you said to the uKhandempemvu? There are the uKhandempemvu going into the tents!' In the face of the subsequent charge, the British line collapsed. Sometimes, to drum up their courage and intimidate the enemy, the warriors would beat their shields with the ends of their spears, producing an ominous rattling noise known as *ingomane*.

Zulu morale

So eager were the warriors to come to grips with the foe that the Zulu army's greatest discipline problem was keeping them in check. Warfare, of course, offered a chance for individuals to prove themselves, to gain the

king's recognition and to profit by plunder, but the reasons for their eagerness went deeper than this. Battle was the final and logical conclusion of the days of preparatory rituals, and the warriors entered it in a heightened emotional state, convinced of their supernatural superiority over the enemy. They were bound to each other by tremendous emotional bonds, and often possessed of a collective anger against the enemy. Several Zulu veterans of the 1879 war described their mental state during combat in terms of a consuming rage – a condition the horrified British interpreted as blood-lust. Certainly the Zulu warrior in battle was trapped in a tunnel-vision world of violence, shaped by powerful forces deep in his psyche and enflamed by the rush of adrenaline. This condition may have been further exaggerated by the practice of taking snuff just before battle, since there are suggestions that

men preparing for combat would have mixed the tobacco with ground cannabis. Certainly, the British soon learned that the younger *amabutho* could be provoked to attack regardless of the wishes of the senior *izinduna*, often with disastrous consequences to the army as a whole.

For most warriors, the experience of battle was one of a brief and merciless exposure to unrestrained violence. In King Shaka's time, the Zulus neither received casualties nor were able to inflict them until they were almost upon their enemy. Any spears flung at them would only reach them at 30 yds range, and by then they had probably already launched their final charge, shields up and stabbing spears drawn back. Most spears could be parried or caught on the large shields, and the shock of impact followed soon after. Henry Francis Fynn described just such a clash he witnessed in 1826:

'. . . both parties, with a tumultuous yell, clashed together, and continued stabbing each other for about three minutes, when both fell back a few paces.

Seeing their losses were about equal, both enemies raised a cry and this was followed by another rush, and they continued closely engaged about twice as long as the first onset, when both parties again drew off. But the enemy's loss had now been the more severe. This urged the Zulus to a final charge. The shrieks now became terrific . . .'*

Combat consisted of a short tussle as each man struggled to catch his opponent off-guard. The Zulu shields were used to batter the enemy, to try to force his own shield across his body, thereby exposing the chest or stomach to an under-arm thrust. A good thrust to the abdomen would cause a horrific injury, putting a man *hors de combat*, and as he fell he was likely to receive further wounds. Fighting was physically exhausting and very bloody, but often quickly resolved, since it was impossible for both sides to stand indefinitely. When an enemy fled, pursuit was likely to be even more costly, as quarter was seldom asked for or given, and in the white heat of battle, it was often impossible to restrain warriors from killing everything they came across, including non-combatants, livestock and even pets. In 1879 King Cetshwayo repeatedly urged his warriors to bring him a live British captive, but the only man they succeeded in capturing was taken at Hlobane mountain, and almost certainly found on the battlefield after the first rush of excitement had cooled.

In 1879 the final charge was preceded by a shower of spears, which struck among the enemy just as the charging warriors reached them, hopefully breaking up their con-

centrations. Although an alert enemy might dodge a single spear, they were effective against tight formations, and were particularly unnerving for horses. At Isandlwana one survivor commented that the spears 'fell like hailstones'. It was in the early battles of 1879 too that the extent to which the Zulus had failed to adapt their tactics to take advantage of their firearms became apparent. They did not alter their traditional tactical approach in any way, but merely used the gun as if it were a superior throwing spear. Many warriors fired just before the final charge; since there was no time then to reload, the majority simply threw down their guns and drew their stabbing spears. As a result, they failed to make the most of the tempting targets offered by the tight British formations, achieving little themselves due to poor marksmanship, but still suffering the full weight of return fire. After these initial experiences, most were disappointed in the performance of their guns, and instead of seeking a new and more effective way of using them, merely fell back on their conventional outlook. In fact, after a significant number of British guns were captured at Isandlwana, Zulu marksmanship did marginally improve, providing a tantalising sign of what might otherwise have been achieved.

Where hand-to-hand fighting did take place in 1879, it was, if anything, more intense than in previous battles, simply because the Zulus had already passed through a horrific ordeal before they reached the enemy. The British fired on them with artillery that was accurate up to 3,000 yds; rockets, Gatling-guns and rifles that were devastating at ranges less than 300 yds. Every stage of the Zulu attack was therefore exposed to an increasing storm of fire, and survivors recalled with horror the effects of British

Ultimately, the Zulu tactics of advancing to the attack in the open was dangerously outmoded in the face of the modern firepower possessed by the British. Here warriors are pinned down, unable to advance, at oNdini (Ulundi).

firepower, which could strike down whole groups of warriors, mangle their bodies and scatter heads and limbs about at will. The Zulu faced this ordeal with remarkable courage, no doubt buoyed up by faith in their preparatory medicines, but inevitably, once they had passed through it, their frustration was unleashed in the final assault. Zulu accounts of the fighting at Isandlwana have an almost hallucinogenic quality, a nightmare succession of images, of twisting, struggling masses of men, of smoke, dust and noise. The final charge was often heralded by a great shout of the national war-cry – in 1879 it was *'uSuthu!'* – and individuals shouted it each time they struck at the enemy. Others shouted the deeper, more ominous cry *'Ngadla!'* – 'I have eaten!' So surreal did this fighting seem that at Isandlwana, young men who had never seen a white man before, and had been told to kill everyone in clothes, stabbed at sacks piled up on supply wagons, while at Khambula the army – who failed to overcome the British defences – retired convinced that they had seen dogs and apes manning the ramparts.

The Zulu army had little in reserve to cope with defeat. Generally, the Zulu were prepared to mount attack after attack, drawing off between each to regroup, until the casualties became too severe or it became obvious that they could not win. So great were the exertions made in these attacks, however, that once the *amabutho* began to retire, it proved impossible to rally them. Often this retreat began in an orderly manner but fell apart under an intense pursuit. *Izinduna* tried valiantly to rally their men, and the 'loins' sometimes attempted to make a stand or cover the

retreat, but such efforts were hopeless in the face of concentrated firepower or mounted pursuit. The British were ruthless in the immediate aftermath of a victory, seeking revenge for Isandlwana, but the Zulu were not shocked by this, since it was a feature of their own warfare. Fleeing warriors were cut down at will, and wounded Zulus killed out of hand. Even when the British took prisoners, they were sometimes shot afterwards. Generally, where warriors were captured, they reacted stoically to their situation, probably realising that once the heat of battle had passed, the British would treat them well.

Post-battle rituals

Descriptions of the aftermath of a battle in which the Zulu were victorious make grim reading. British troops returning to Isandlwana found their dead partly stripped of clothing, and badly cut about. Many were undoubtedly repeatedly stabbed in the frenzy of combat, while others had been stabbed again after death in a practice known as *hlomula*. This had its origins in the hunt for dangerous game – lion or buffalo – when each man in the hunting party was entitled to claim some part of the glory of triumph by jabbing his spear into the corpse. The custom

Having expended most of their energy in attack, the Zulus had few reserves to offer in retreat, and were particularly vulnerable in the face of a determined pursuit. This sketch of the battle of oNdini shows the various amakhanda on the surrounding heights already in flames before the battle has ended. (National Army Museum)

was only followed in battle when fighting a particularly brave foe, although the British did not appreciate the implied honour. Furthermore, when a Zulu killed another in battle, he was tainted by the *umnyama* he had unleashed, and it was necessary to begin the complex cleansing rites by stripping some clothing from the corpse and putting it on. In battles against African enemies, this usually meant the *umutsha*, while in 1879 the Zulu stripped jackets from the British dead. They were required to wear them until they had been completely purified. As part of the same rite, and due to a widespread belief that the soul of the dead warrior escaped through the stomach, they disembowelled the man they had killed. If the stomach cavity was not opened, the slayer would be haunted by *umnyama* unleashed by the trapped and vengeful spirit, and his own body would swell, eventually sending him mad. In the immediate aftermath of Isandlwana, the battlefield resembled an abattoir, human and animal corpses jumbled up together, 'and the green grass was wet with the running blood and the veld was slippery, for it was covered with the brains and entrails of the slain'.

Anything found on the bodies was considered as spoils of war, and from the British dead the Zulus took watches, coins and other possessions according to their fancy. Military spoils were of course much in demand, particularly rifles and powder, but swords and revolvers were taken more as souvenirs, since the Zulu considered their own weapons more practicable. The field guns over-run at Isandlwana were taken away but never put into service.

Enemy dead were left on the battlefield. Indeed, once passions had cooled, the stiffening corpse was regarded as a source of *umnyama*, not to be touched if at all possible. Zulu dead were given the most notional of burials: friends and relatives sought out their kinsmen, and dragged the body into a convenient hole – a nearby grain-pit or a donga (erosion gully) – or simply covered it with a shield. The warrior was to some extent prepared for death by the rituals he had undergone, and what mattered was not his body, but his spirit, which would be respected by ceremonies undertaken at his family homestead. The wounded too had to rely on the goodwill of friends and relatives to find them and carry them away. This was not an easy task following a victory on home soil – it took ten days for the first of the army to return to oNdini after Isandlwana because the wounded were so plentiful – and it must have led to slow and agonising journeys when battles were

fought in far-off places. After a defeat, it was even worse, for any Zulu helping away a wounded man were helpless in the face of a determined pursuit. Physical obstacles then became insurmountable, and even the most dedicated kinsmen had little choice but to abandon their charges. After the battle of Gingindlovu, the British found scores of dead in the long grass along the banks of the Nyezane river; the wounded had been carried thus far, but could not be carried across, and were left to their fate.

MEDICAL CARE

Zulu wounded had little hope of specialist treatment until they returned home. A life in the open had taught them that pain had to be endured, and open wounds were bound up with grass. Wooden splints were used to support fractures. The *izinyanga* made little distinction between the body and the spirit, both of which needed attention after a campaign, and treatment of wounds consisted largely of frequent washing and the application of various herbal remedies to combat infection. Most of the wounds endured in pre-Colonial campaigns consisted of cuts, piercing injuries and slashes and, providing no major internal organs were damaged, these could be stitched up

The realities of death at the hands of the Zulu were decidedly inglorious, as this surprisingly frank sketch of the body of the Prince Imperial – naked and riddled with stab wounds – suggests. (Rai England Collection)

A graphic representation of the effects of concentrated rifle-fire: the corpses of men of the uThulwana and its associated amabutho *piled below the barricades at Rorke's Drift.*

Right: The terrible injuries inflicted on the Zulu in the war of 1879 are demonstrated in these studies of bones injured by Martini-Henry bullets, from a British doctor's notebook.

with a good chance of recovery, as an account of the treatment meted out to Diyikana kaHlakanyana, wounded in one of King Dingane's campaigns, suggests:

'He had three large wounds on the body. One was on the head, extending from above the right eye to the ear; another was on the chest, from above the nipple to the right shoulder; another on the stomach, to the side and round to the back where the ribs end. That one had to be stitched up with sinew; his intestines were thoroughly washed and pushed back inside . . . That is how he survived.'

There are numerous accounts of warriors surviving multiple wounds in this way, testifying to both the hardiness of the men themselves, and to the skill of the *izinyanga*. In 1879, however, the Zulu were exposed to a horrifying range of new and terrible injuries; blast injuries from shell-fire, burns from rockets, wounds from heavy-calibre bullets, sword-slashes and bayonet thrusts. Many warriors survived them to a remarkable degree – one British veteran met a Zulu at the end of the war who had suffered no fewer than eleven bullet wounds at Isandlwana alone – but this was largely a matter of chance. The relatively high velocity of the British Martini-Henry meant that its bullets clipped neatly through flesh but had a shattering effect on bone. Flesh wounds could be washed regularly and closed up, but there was no viable treatment for smashed limbs, beyond amputation. Although there are references to Zulus surviving after damaged and exposed bones had been cut away, there was no anaesthetic available, and the chances of survival were slim. Head wounds and serious body-wounds were almost always fatal, and the warriors who survived to impress white travellers with their gruesome scars were usually those who had been lucky enough to suffer only flesh-wounds.

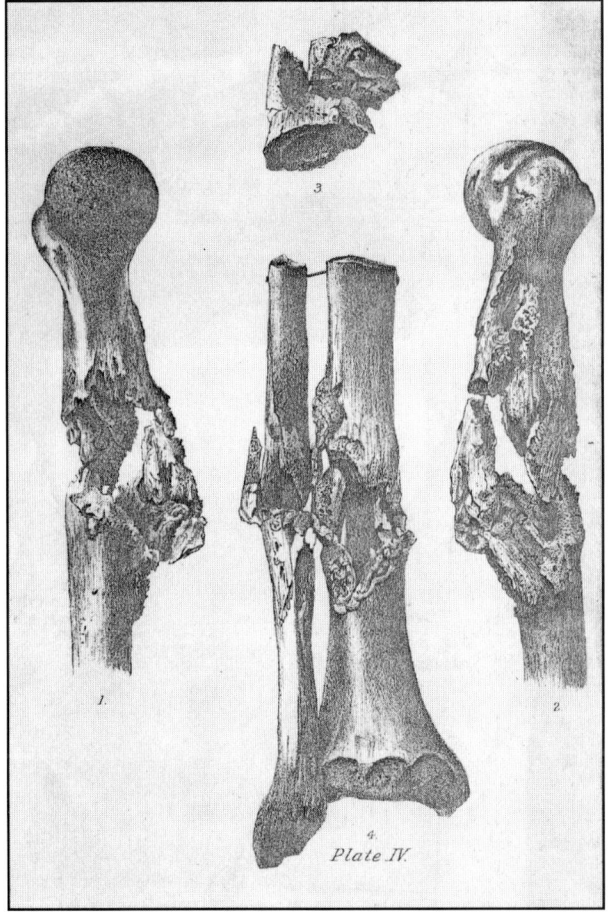

Plate IV.

AFTER THE CAMPAIGN

When the army returned from a campaign, it was required to report to the king. Those who had killed in battle or had *hlomula*'d a corpse – they were known as *izinxweleha* – and those who had been wounded were first separated off, as they were deeply contaminated by the blood shed in violent acts. They were taken to homesteads appointed by the king, where they were required to undergo various ceremonies before they could enter the royal presence. Still wearing the clothing of the men they had killed, and carrying their blood-stained spears, they were marched every day to a nearby river to bathe. They wore sprigs of wild asparagus in their hair as a sign of their condition. Medicines taken from the necklaces they wore in battle were prepared for them, and they were required to *ncinda* – dip their fingers into the bowl of liquid and suck it off the finger tips. They then squirted it through their teeth in the direction of the enemy, chanting 'Come out, evil spirit, fall evil spirit'. This process was repeated over several days. The wounded went through a similar process, and had their injuries treated.

Once this had been accomplished, those who had killed, and who were known either as *ingwazi* ('stabber') or *iqawe* ('hero'), cut and stripped the bark from long wands of willow wood and, together with those wounded who were able, rejoined the army assembled at the 'great place'. Here all warriors were required to undergo a final *ncinda* ceremony under the watchful eye of one of the king's most trusted *izinyanga*. The king himself was once again smeared with powerful medicines to prevent him from being polluted when the army was at last brought before him. The *amabutho* paraded before him in a ceremony known as *ukupumpatisa inkosi* – the 'hoodwinking of the

A solitary corpse on the battlefield of oNdini, 4 July 1879. Note the musket and powder-horn. (Sherard Foresters' Museum, Nottingham)

king'. The warriors chanted songs of victory, while their *izinduna* regaled the king with accounts of how each had performed in the fighting.

Rewards and punishments

If the Zulu warrior was generally content to fight for the king for no reason other than fulfilling the duty of service expected of him, there was nevertheless the possibility of more tangible forms of reward. In the early days of the kingdom, in particular, when most warfare consisted of either enlarging the kingdom's borders or of aggressive campaigning beyond them, most expeditions resulted in looting. Securing the enemy's cattle was a prime objective, and it was not uncommon for herds numbering thousands of head to be brought back to Zululand to enrich the national herd. Much of the kingdom's wealth in cattle can be traced to the successful campaigning of the period 1816–24. Captured animals belonged to the state, and were kept at the various royal homesteads, but the king had the right to give some away to individuals who had distinguished themselves. When the army was called together to review the campaign, regimental *izinduna* would call out individuals who had distinguished themselves, and recount their heroic deeds. The king would then award them a number of cattle according to their achievements; Shaka, for whom courage in battle was an outstanding virtue, was generous, and awarded as many as ten head to heroes who had fought well. Others received less, according to their deeds. Since it was difficult for unmarried men to accumulate cattle in their own right, such rewards had a very real effect on their material well-being and standing. It was also possible that men who showed consistent courage and ability might be made *induna*, thereby beginning a process of promotion that might eventually see them appointed to the command of a newly *buta*'d *ibutho*. These were the *izilomo*, the men favoured by the king.

The king might also award other tokens of approval, of less practical value, but immensely prestigious nonetheless. Particularly valued were arm-bands, made out of brass and shaped like the cuff of a gauntlet, called *izingxotha* (sing. *ingxotha*). These were made from slabs of brass imported from Mozambique, and were decorated with raised ridges and nodules. They were worn singly, on the right wrist only. Their significance was not purely military, but they were awarded by the king personally to anyone who had particularly distinguished himself in the royal service in some capacity. *Izikhulu* often wore them by right of their hereditary rank; the *izilomo* had to be given permission to wear them.

Medical support: an inyanga, **wearing the horns and gourds which symbolised his role as a herbalist.**

Award of battle honours

When the army returned from a campaign, the king would discuss with his *izinduna* which *ibutho* had played the most prominent part in the fighting. Those regiments who had challenged one another would be summoned again, the challenges recalled, and their performance assessed. All of those within the selected regiment who had actually killed one of the enemy would be given the right to cut *iziqu*, necklaces of small blocks made from their wands of willow-wood, which served as a public recognition of their heroic service. In 1879, for example, it was generally agreed that the uMbonambi *ibutho* had been the first to break through the British lines at Isandlwana, and their heroes were given the right to wear the *iziqu*. These *iziqu* were highly prized, and were worn on important occasions by all warriors who had won the right. If the same warriors distinguished themselves again in a later campaign, they might be allowed to add new beads to their *iziqu*; anyone wearing beads to which he had no claim, however, was despised as a charlatan, and might even be killed for insulting the king's bounty. Other, lesser, badges of royal approval included the right, given either to an entire regiment or to individuals, to wear particular articles of regalia, approved by the king. Most commonly these included small bunches or single feathers of the scarlet lourie, which was otherwise reserved for men of high rank.

If heroes were praised, however, those who had flinched in the face of combat were subjected to an unpleasant ordeal. King Shaka, it is said, regularly had cowards killed off; those who were identified were singled out before the entire army and stabbed in the armpit. (There is still a bush near Shaka's kwaBulawayo homestead known as the *isihlala samagwala* – the cowards' bush, where such executions are said to have occurred.) Some of these stories are undoubtedly exaggerated, but Shaka was certainly a martinet, and such executions must have served to reinforce a military ethic when the fate of the emergent nation depended on the discipline and unity of the army. Such draconian measures were not so available to Shaka's successors, and by the 1870s, the coward was more likely to be publicly humiliated. Even so, his lot was hardly enviable: his misdeeds were reported to the king in front of the assembled army, and he was directed to sit aside with others who had performed badly. When cooked meat was produced to feed the army, that for the cowards was taken to them on a pot-sherd, but dipped into a bowl of water before it was handed to them. This was a gesture of contempt, and often a warrior who had performed well would dash the water into a coward's face, knowing that he dared not respond. Cowards were liable to be abandoned by their lovers, since brave men were believed to make better husbands, and girls who were seen with a known coward were liable to be taunted with shouts of, 'is it so, then, that girls court one another?' The disgrace was serious and damaging, but it was not necessarily permanent, since it was believed that it served to stimulate a man to fight better on a future occasion. If a known coward particularly distinguished himself in a subsequent fight, the king, on hearing of the matter, would say 'Is it so? Then he has left the pot-sherd of the cowards. Let him no longer eat the meat of the cowards, but eat the meat of the heroes instead.'

DISASTER AND DEFEAT

In the aftermath of a normal campaign, the Zulu army would expect to disperse after the necessary ceremonies had been completed. The warriors were usually spent, and would need a rest to recover, and they would be needed, in any case, to pick up the threads of the civilian lives which they had only temporarily abandoned. They returned home to tell their families of their adventures, to replace their damaged costumes, and perhaps to re-haft and sharpen their spears ready for future campaigning. There was no prospect of a formal retirement, although married *amabutho* played less of a role as each year went by. It was not unknown for men in their fifties and sixties to take to the field, but their effectiveness was inevitably limited, and by that time more and more men were content to stay at home, to enjoy the pleasures of their herds and families, and to sit in the shade, drinking beer and talking over the great deeds of their youth.

The 1879 war did not differ fundamentally from this pattern: after the battles of January, the king allowed the men to return to their homes until a further wave of fighting appeared imminent at the end of March. After Khambula and Gingindlovu – both defeats – this need was all the more pressing. Nevertheless, the army still reassembled in June, to make one last gesture of defiance, at the doorstep of the *komkhulu* itself. This persistence was quite extraordinary, given the appalling number of casualties that greeted each new battle. The warriors were prepared to face the ordeal time and again, until at last they accepted that they had no hope of winning; at the battle of oNdini, on 4 July, they were finally broken, never to reassemble. The king fled to the bush, and was hunted down by British Dragoons, and taken into exile. The great complex of *amakhanda* on the Mahlabathini plain was burnt to the ground, a fate which had already befallen many elsewhere in the country. The sacred coil which held

The passions of war long cooled: a poignant photo taken some time in the 1930s, of Dugald Macphail (with medals, right) who, as a Quartermaster in the Buffalo Border Guard, had survived Isandlwana, and who later served in the 1906 rebellion, discussing the battle with an anonymous Zulu veteran who had been on the other side. (Local History Museum, Durban)

the nation together was burnt and the nation did indeed fall apart.

For most ordinary Zulus, the end of the war at first came as a relief. They were exhausted, and the nation had suffered enough. British observers noted that soon after the hostilities had ceased, Zulu men, who no longer needed to wait for the king's permission, began to marry freely. The habit of wearing the *isicoco* – the 'king's ring' – began to die out. Nevertheless, although the post-war settlement deliberately sought to exclude the Zulu royal house, and to recognise instead the independence of selected *izikhulu*, many Zulus still remained loyal to the king. Civil war between royalist and anti-royalist factions characterised the decade following the war. Those who supported the king still thought of themselves as belonging to their pre-war *amabutho*, although with no *amakhanda* to house them and no means available to the royal house to support them, this allegiance remained largely nominal. The mainspring which held the structure of the kingdom together had been broken, and the armies of the civil war period became increasingly regional in character. *Amaviyo* rather than *amabutho* became the standard battlefield unit. Men no longer mustered on a regular basis merely to take part in an imminent fight. Nevertheless, the ethic of the old Zulu army continued to influence the outlook, strategy and tactics of all sides, until

in 1906 the last desperate revolt against Colonial rule – which began in Natal and had only limited support in Zululand – proved once and for all that the out look of Shaka's day was hopelessly outdated in the world of Maxim machine-guns.

THE PLATES

A: Ceremonial dress
The basic ingredients of the full ceremonial regalia of the younger *amabutho* remained largely unchanged from King Shaka's time to the 1879 Anglo-Zulu War.1 The *umtusha* loin covering, consisting of a narrow belt of hide with an oblong of cowhide, *ibeshu*, over the buttocks, and an apron of fur twisted around a central core so as to resemble tails, called *isinene*, was common to most regiments young or old; 2 So, too, were the dense body ornaments, made from bunches of cow-tails attached to a necklace so as to hang to the waist at front and the knees at the back; 3 Headbands were made by stitching otter or leoparkskin into a roll, and stuffing it with a bull-rush or dried cow-dung, whilst 'tails' – made in the same fashion as for the *isinene* – were often attached behind; 4 the *amaphovela* headress, two stiff pieces of hide with cowtails tied to the tips, were a unique part of

the uniform of the unmarried men; **5** as were the bunches of *sakabuli* feathers tied to porcupine quills and fixed inside the headband, and the predominantly black shields.

B: War dress, c. 1879

1 A young warrior of the iNgobamakhosi *ibutho* in the typical war-dress of the 1879 period. Although some warriors retained part of their ceremonial regalia in battle, most younger men wore nothing but a loin covering and a necklace of charms to ward off evil; this man also has a snuff container around his neck, and a snuff-spoon in his ear. Although by 1879 a large number of Zulus carried some form of firearm – like the outdated percusson model carried here, together with a leather bag for shot and a powder-horn – they continued to place more faith in their traditional weapons. **2** The smaller *umbumbuluzo* war-shield, shown here, was more popular than the original *isihlangu*, although both types were carried, even within the same regiment. Offensive weapons consisted of; **3** stabbing spear – an expertly crafted blade set into a wooden haft, and either bound round with animal fibre and covered with a tube of hide from a calf's tail, or sealed with split cane; **4** lighter throwing spears; **5** a variety of knobkerries, some decorated with copper or brass wire; **6** the axe was less common, and largely carried as a prestige weapon by men of rank.

C: Zulu regalia

1 The chief distinguishing mark of the married man was the *isicoco*, or headring. This was made by; **(a)** binding a fibre into the hair, **(b)** shaving the head around it, **(c)** then covering it with gum, which was then highly polished. **2** On ceremonial occasions, senior *amabutho* wore a distinctive costume which typically consisted of a waist-kilt of twisted tails, a headband of otter skin, and the tail feathers of the Blue Crane. Their shields – the type shown here is the full-sized *isihlangu* – were predominantly white. **3** Men of the highest rank were distinguished by crane feathers, bunches of scarlet and green lourie feathers, and; **4** if very senior, necklaces made of large blood-red beads and slivers of bone, carved to resemble claws; **5** Tangible signs of royal approval or acknowledged bravery in battle were a brass armband, *ingxotha*, worn on the right wrist only; and **6** a necklace of interlocking wooden beads, known as *iziqu*.

D: The warshield

The true warshield was the property of the Zulu state, and issued only when men were actively in the service of the king. **1** The shields were cut from the hides of carefully matched cattle, two from each hide so that minor variations of colouring between shields were inevitable. **2** They were strengthened by strips of hide threaded through parallel rows of slits cut down the middle. **3** A stick was then pushed through these strips at the back; **4** the top of the stick was shaped to receive a piece of fur as a decoration. **5** The shield was held by the stick, by a handle made from the hide strips, or both. **6a** The original *isihlangu* shield effectively covered a warrior from shoulder to ankle; **6b** although the later *umbubuluzo* was smaller and easier to carry. **7** Although the uniformity of shield colourings within an *ibutho* was less consistent by 1879, and several regiments are associated with a number of colours, it is possible to make a cautious identification of some of these. Top row; **(a)** King Shaka's war-shield, **(b)** war-shield of uThulwana *ibutho*, 1879. Middle row; **(d)** uMxapho *ibutho* (conjectured), and **(e&f)** two patterns associated with uKhandempemvu *ibutho*, 1879. Bottom row; **(g)** uMbonambi *ibutho*, **(h)** uNokhenke *ibutho*, **(i)** iNgobamakhosi *ibutho*, all 1879.

E: Cadet training

Young warriors undergoing their cadet-ship in an *ikhanda* practise stick-fighting – which was both a means of improving fighting techniques, demonstrating manliness, and resolving arguments. They are watched by one of the king's *izinduna*, right, and two older youths, left, from the age-group immediately above them, who have already been enrolled into an *ibutho*. Small shields such as those shown here were for everyday protection, and would be carried in most of the dancing displays which served to teach the warriors co-ordination within the ranks.

F: On the march, c. 1879

A Zulu army on the march. It advanced to the front in two parallel columns of regiments, with *izindibi* boys carrying mats or driving cattle for slaughter on the flanks. Individual scouts would spy out the enemy's movements for many miles in front of the army, whilst between them and the main body was a denser screen which acted as a vanguard. Here one of these scouts returns to report what he has seen to a senior *induna*, raising his arm and crouching as a mark of respect; from the 1850s, firearms were increasingly common within the army, and by 1879 a number of individual chiefs and *izinduna* had acquired horses from white traders.

G: Final preparations for battle

Having reached the enemy's position, it was the usual Zulu practise to draw the assembled army up into a circle, or *umkhumbi*, to hear a final address and instructions from the senior *izinduna*. The *izinyanga*, the doctors who specialised in medicines designed to protect men in times of war, went amongst the warriors spattering them with *intelezi* medicines. The importance of these rituals was fully accepted by the Zulu, who believed that failure in battle would result without them.

H: The 'beast's horns'
The favourite Zulu attack formation, the 'beast's horns', in action in a running fight with the Boers in 1838. The 'chest', usually composed of senior warriors, advanced rapidly on the enemy's front. When fighting opponents armed with firearms, the warriors usually deployed in open lines, with wide gaps between them, and by 1879 they were adept at skirmishing, running quickly forward from cover to cover. The flanking parties or 'horns', usually consisting of young, unmarried *amabutho*, rushed out on either side in an attempt to surround the enemy. If circumstances permitted, it was not unknown for one 'horn' to mask its advance in broken terrain, as here, so as to take the enemy by surprise. Although in 1838 the Zulus faced an enemy armed with firearms for the first time, they recovered quickly from any shock, and in an open fight were more than capable of holding their own. Nor was the Boer's skilled horsemanship a particular advantage, since in broken terrain the Zulus could move almost as swiftly as even the most skilled horsemen.

I: Hand-to-hand fighting
The shock of battle. Throughout the kingdom's history, Zulu military success was dependant upon the ability to come to close-quarters in order to employ proven hand-to-hand fighting techniques. In the early days, this was devastatingly effective – as in this reconstruction of one of Shaka's battles – but by 1879 the advent of a foe armed with sophisticated firearms rendered such an aproach costly and usually futile. The experience of fighting itself was short, but fierce and savage, a bloody eye-ball to eye-ball contest with stabbing weapons which inflicted horrific injuries. It was in such conditions that the combined use of the shield and stabbing spear had been perfected.

J: Aftermath of Isandlwana, 1879
Even a successful battle usually resulted in a large number of Zulu wounded, and there was little in the way of immediate medical treatment available. Open wounds were bound up with grass, and badly wounded were helped from the field by their friends and relatives. The dead were given a makeshift burial in dongas, ant-bear holes or nearby grain-pits, or simply covered over with a shield. The fate of the enemy dead was a grisly one; many had been repeatedly stabbed in the excitement of combat itself, and often stabbed again by those coming up behind in a practise which was a macabre testament to the ferocity with which they had fought. The pre-combat rituals had complex counterparts to be observed after battle, and these began immediately when warriors who had killed stripped some of the clothing from their victims, and put it on themselves. When a British camp or convoy fell to the Zulus, it was thoroughly ransacked, the Zulus carrying away not only everything of military value, but countless exotic items which caught their fancy.

K: Purification from the blood of battle
After a successful battle such as Isandlwana, those who had been spiritually contaminated by contact with spilt blood – those who had killed an enemy, or been wounded

A modern shield-maker at work in traditional dress.

themselves – had to undergo complex purification rituals before they were able to rejoin civilian society. Here the *izinxweleha*, those who had killed, troop down to a river to bathe under the watchful eye of an *inyanga*. They are still wearing items of clothing taken from their victims, and carrying their blood-stained weapons, which they must do until the cermonies are complete. They are wearing sprigs of wild asparagus in their hair, as a badge of their condition. These rituals took several days to perform, and involved regular bathing and sprinkling with protective medicines. The army could not assemble before the king until all were purified, in case their contamination affected him, and brought misfortune on the nation.

L: The return of peace, late 1879

Old age meant a gradual retirement from active service to the king. Individuals continued to muster with their *ibutho* as long as they felt able, but married regiments were only summoned in any case for the annual umKhosi ceremony or in times of national emergency. Since the Zulu army

A Zulu ibutho today, recalling past glories on the Isandlwana battlefield.

was no more than the combined strength of Zulu manhood under arms, such a retirement brought no great change of lifestyle, and a warrior faced his twilight years secure in the knowledge that his past service and advancing years ensured him the respect of not only his immediate family, but his age-mates and juniors too. It was a time to enjoy one's cattle, and talk over old battles around the beer-pot.

At the end of the 1879 war, a British officer, Captain Molyneux, was astonished at the lack of rancour which the Zulus displayed towards those who only a few weeks before had been enemies; he was, however, amazed at the number of conspicuous injuries which many Zulus had sustained in defence of their country, and survived with only rudimentary treatment. Their stories encapsulated the experience of countless warriors, and the bitter truth that in the last resort the courage which had sustained their fighting spirit from the time of King Shaka was an inadequate protection in the face of modern firepower.

PLACES TO VISIT

There are a number of interesting collections of Zulu possessions in both South Africa and the UK. Indeed, because the British looted large numbers of Zulu weapons as souvenirs in the 1879 war, much of the more interesting material is now in the UK. The museums of most regiments who fought in the war have a few things relating to it, though they are not always accurately labelled. The following list includes the most important collections:

United Kingdom

Brecon, Wales, Royal Regiment of Wales Museum Contains a large number of relics relating to the battles of Isandlwana and Rorke's Drift, including a shield recovered at Rorke's Drift, *izingxotha*, spears and chief' staffs.

Brighton Museum Includes *isihlangu* shield recovered at oNdini.

Chatham, Royal Engineers Museum A small shield taken from oNdini by Lt. Chard, and a magnificent example of a charm necklace.

Osborne House, Isle of White Swiss Cottage includes three *izihlangu* shields, mounted as trophies, with spears and non-Zulu artefacts, as presented to Queen Victoria.

Taunton Museum Relics relating to 13th LI experience in Anglo-Zulu war, including an *isihlangu* shield.

South Africa

Eshowe, Zululand Historical Museum Housed in a historical curiosity, a turreted fort built as a barracks for the Zululand Native Police in the 1880s, this museum includes displays on Zulu custom, life and weapons.

Isandlwana Small museum of relics from the battle, including Zulu shield and weapons.

Killie Campbell Africana Museum, Durban Collection of Zulu artefacts, including weapons, *ingxotha* and *iziqu*.

KwaZulu Cultural Museum, oNdini This museum is built close to King Cetshwayo's oNdini homestead, which was destroyed by the British in 1879 and has partly been restored. An excellent opportunity to see what life in an *ikhanda* was like.

Ladysmith, Block House Museum Private museum including excellent reconstruction of Zulu warrior in full regalia.

Local History Museum, Durban Exhibits relating to early history of contact between settlers and Zulus, including a model of King Dingane's eMgungundlovu residence.

eMgungundlovu Part of King Dingane's *komkhulu*, destroyed by fire in 1838, has been rebuilt, and provides a fascinating insight into the mechanics of an *ikhanda*.

Natal Museum, Pietermaritzburg Excellent displays on Natal history and African culture, including weapons, head-dress etc.

Rorke's Drift Museum Excellent museum interpreting famous battle from British and Zulu viewpoints.

Talana Museum, Dundee Collection of spears and battlefield debris from Anglo-Zulu war.

Bibliography

Bryant, A.T., *The Zulu People: As They Were Before The White Man Came* (Pietermaritzburg, 1949)

Castle, I., and Knight, I., *Fearful Hard Times: The Siege and Relief of Eshowe* (London, 1994)

Fynn, Henry Francis, *The Diary of Henry Francis Fynn* (eds. Stuart and Malcolm (Pietermaritzburg, 1950)

Gardiner, A., *Narrative of a Journey To The Zoolu Country* (London, 1836)

Guy, Jeff, *The Destruction of the Zulu Kingdom* (London, 1979)

Isaacs, Nathanial, *Travels and Adventures in Eastern Africa (Natal)* (London, 1936)

Knight, I., *Brave Men's Blood: The Epic of the Zulu War* (London, 1990)

Knight, I., *The Zulus* (Osprey Elite Series, 1989)

Knight, I., *Zulu: The Battles of Isandlwana and Rorke's Drift* (London, 1992)

Knight, I., *Nothing Remains But To Fight: The Defence of Rorke's Drift* (London, 1993)

Laband, John, *Kingdom In Crisis: The Zulu Response To The British Invasion of 1879* (Manchester, 1992)

Laband, John, and Thompson, Paul, *Kingdom and Colony at War* (Pietermaritzburg, 1990)

Samuelson, R.C., *Long Long Ago* (Durban, 1929)

Webb, C. de B., and Wright, J.B. (eds.), *The James Stuart Archive*, Vols 1–4 (Pietermaritzburg and Durban, 1976, 1979, 1982, 1986)

Webb, C. de B., and Wright, J.B. (eds.), *A Zulu King Speaks: Statements made by Cetshwayo kaMpande on the History and Customs of His People* (Pietermaritzburg and Durban, 1978)

Notes sur les planches en couleurs

A Eléments de base du costume de cérémonie complet du jeune *amabutho*; **1** Le pagne *umutsha*; **2** Denses décorations du corps, constituées de bouquets de queues de vaches attachés à un collier de manière à pendre jusqu'à la taille devant et jusqu'aux genoux derrière; **3** Les serre-tête étaient fabriqués en cousant des peaux de loutre ou de léopard en boudin que l'on remplissait de massettes de roseaux ou de bouse de vache séchée alors que des 'queues' (fabriquées de la même manière que l'*isinene*) étaient souvent attachées dans le dos; **4** le couvre-chef *amapovela*, deux morceaux de peau rigides avec des queues de vache attachées aux extrémités; **5** bouquets de plumes *sakabuli* attachées à des piquants de porc-épic et fixés à l'intérieur du serre-tête.

B1 Un jeune guerrier des iNgobamakhosi *ibutho* portant le costume de guerre typique de la période 1879. Bien qu'en 1879 beaucoup de Zoulous possédaient une arme à feu, comme le modèle vétuste à percussion illustré ici, accompagné d'un sac de cuir pour les plombs et une corne à poudre, ils continuaient de faire plus confiance à leurs armes traditionnelles; **2** Le bouclier de guerre *umbhumbulosu*, de plus petite taille, était plus populaire que l'*isihlangu* d'origine, mais on voyait les deux, même dans le même régiment. Les armes offensives comportaient; **3** une lance poignard; **4** des lances plus légères; **5** diverses massues, certaines décorés de fils de laiton ou de cuivre; **6** la hache était moins courante et souvent portée comme arme de prestige par les hommes de haut rang.

C1 Les hommes mariés portaient le *isococo* ou anneau de tête. Il était fait de la manière suivante, **(a)** on tressait des fibres dans les cheveux, **(b)** on rasait les cheveux autour, **(c)** puis on le recouvrait de gomme, que l'on polissait longuement; **2** Durant les cérémonies, les *amabutho* sénior portaient un costume distinctif qui était typiquement composé d'un pagne de queues entrelacées, d'un serre-tête de peau de loutre et des plumes de la queue des grues de paradis. Leur bouclier était à dominante de blanc. **3** Les hommes du plus haut rang se distinguaient par des plumes de grue, des bouquets de plumes de touraco écarlates et vertes et; **4** s'ils étaient très expérimentés, par des colliers de grosses perles rouge sang et de morceaux d'os sculptés pour ressembler à des griffes; **5** Les signes tangibles de l'approbation royale ou d'un acte de bravoure durant le combat étaient un brassard de cuivre, *ingxotha*, porté uniquement au poignet droit et **6** un collier de perles de bois entrelacées, nommé *iziqu*.

D1 Les boucliers de guerre étaient découpés dans des peaux de bétail soigneusement choisies; **2** renforcés par des bandes de cuir lacées dans des rangs parallèles de fentes découpées au milieu; **3** On enfonçait alors un bâton dans ces bandes àl'arrière; **4** le haut du bâton était sculpté pour recevoir un morceau de fourrure comme décoration. **5** Le bouclié était tenu par le bâton, par une poignée faite à partir des bandes de cuir, ou les deux. **6a-b** longueur des boucliers; **7** Identification des boucliers rang supérieur **(a)** bouclier de guerre du Roi Shaka **(b)** bouclier de guerre de uThulwana *ibutho* et **(c)** uDloko *ibutho*, 1879. Rang du milieu **(d)** uMxapho *ibutho* (imaginé) et **(e & f)** deux styles associés à uKhandempemvu *ibutho*, 1879. Rang inférieur **(g)** uMbonami *ibutho* **(h)** uNokhenke *ibutho* **(i)** iNgobamakhosi *ibutho*, tous 1879.

E Jeunes guerriers à l'entraînement dans un exercice de combat au bâton *ikhanda*. Ils sont observés par l'un des *izinduna* du roi, à droite, et deux jeunes gens plus âgés, à gauche, faisant partie du groupe d'âge immédiatement supérieur au leur et qui ont déjà été enrôlés dans un *ibutho*.

F Armée zoulou en marche. Elle avançait vers le front en deux colonnes de régiments parallèles, avec des garçons *izindibi* portant des nattes ou gardant du bétail destiné à être abattu sur les flancs. Des éclaireurs surveillaient les mouvements de l'ennemi à plusieurs kilomètres en avant de l'armée et entre eux et le corps principal se trouvait un écran plus dense qui jouait le rôle d'avant-garde. Ici, l'un de ces éclaireurs vient annoncer à un induna sénior ce qu'il a vu. Il soulève le bras et s'accroupit pour marquer son respect.

G Ayant atteint la position de l'ennemi, la coutume habituelle des Zoulous était de rassembler l'armée en un cercle, ou um*khumbi* pour écouter un dernier discours et des instructions des *izinduna* expérimentés. Les *izinyanga*, docteurs spécialisés dans les médecines conçues pour protéger les hommes en temps de guerre, parcouraient les rangs des guerriers et les aspergeaient de médecines *intelezi*.

H La formation d'attaque préférée des Zoulous ou 'cornes de la bête' en action durant un combat à la course contre les Boers en 1838. Le 'poitrail', généralement composé de guerriers chevronnés, avançait rapidement sur le front ennemi alors que les flancs ou 'cornes' généralement composées de jeunes am*abutho* célibataires couraient de chaque côté pour tenter d'encercler l'ennemi.

I Le choc du combat. L'expérience du combat lui-même était courte mais violente et sauvage, un combat sanguinaire corps-à-corps avec des armes poignards qui infligeaient d'horribles blessures. C'est dans ces conditions que l'usage combiné du bouclier et de la lance poignard fut perfectionné.

J Même durant un combat victorieux il y avait de nombreux blessés Zoulous et les traitements médicaux immédiats étaient peu nombreux. Les plaies ouvertes étaient refermées avec des liens végétaux et les blessés graves étaient évacués avec l'aide de leurs amis et parents. Les morts recevaient une sépulture de fortune dans des ravins, des trous de fourmiliers ou des fosses à grain proches, ou encore étaient tout simplement recouverts d'un bouclier. Le sort des morts ennemis était toujours horrible.

K Après un combat victorieux comme à Isandlwana, les guerriers dont l'esprit avait été contaminé par un contact avec du sang versé (ceux qui avaient tué un ennemi ou qui avaient été blessés eux-mêmes) devaient se soumettre à de complexes rituels de purification avant de pouvoir rejoindre la société civile.

L La vieillesse signifiait un retrait progressif du service actif du roi. Les individus continuaient à servir dans leur ibuth*o* aussi longtemps qu'ils se sentaient capables de

Farbtafeln

A Unerläßliche Stücke der zeremoniellen Insignien eines jüngeren *amabutho*; **1** Der *umutsha*-Lendenschurz; **2** dichter Körperschmuck, der aus Büscheln von Kuhschwänzen besteht, die an einem Halsband befestigt sind, so daß sie vorne bis zur Taille und im Rücken bis zu den Knien reichen; **3** Stirnbänder bestanden aus Otter- bzw. Leopardenhaut, die zu einer Rolle zusammengenäht und dann mit Rohr oder getrocknetem Kuhmist ausgestopft wurde. Die "Schwänze" - die auf die gleiche Art wie bei den *isinene* gemacht wurden - waren oft hinten befestigt; **4** der *amapovela*-Kopfschmuck, bei dem es sich um zwei steife Stücke Tierhaut handelt, an denen Kuhschwänze angebracht sind; **5** Büschel von *sakabuli*-Federn, die an die Stacheln von Stachelschweinen gebunden und auf der Innenseite des Stirnbandes befestigt werden.

B1 Ein junger Krieger des iNgobamakhosi-*ibutho* im typischen Kriegsschmuck der Zeit um 1879. Zwar hatten viele Zulus 1879 bereits irgendeine Feuerwaffe - wie das hier abgebildete, altmodische Zündgewehr mit Ledertasche für Munition und einem Schießpulverbehälter - doch vertrauten sie weiterhin eher auf ihre traditionellen Waffen. **2** Der kleinere *umbhumbulosu*-Kriegsschild war beliebter als der ursprüngliche *isihlangu*, obgleich beide Arten vertreten waren - manchmal sogar innerhalb des gleichen Regiments. Die Offensivwaffen bestanden aus: **3** Stichspeer; **4** leichtere Wurfspeere; **5** verschiedene Kirris, von denen einige mit Kupfer- bzw. Messingdraht geschmückt sind; **6** die Streitaxt war weniger geläufig und wurde meistens als Prestige-Waffe von hochstehenden Männern getragen.

C1 Verheiratete Männer trugen den *isicoco*, den Kopfring. Dieser wurde folgendermaßen gefertigt: **(a)** Zunächst wird eine Faser ins Haar geflochten, **(b)** dann wird das Haar außen herum rasiert, **(c)** dann wird der Kopf mit Gummi bestrichen, das anschließend auf Hochglanz poliert wurde. **2** Bei Zeremonien trugen ältere *amabutho* ein charakteristisches Kostüm, das typischerweise aus einem Taillenrock mit gedrehten Schwänzen bestand, einem Stirnband aus Otterfell und den Schwanzfedern des blauen Kranichs. Ihr Schild war vornehmlich weiß. **3** Die Männer des höchsten Rangs zeichneten sich durch Kranenfedern aus sowie Büschel scharlachroter und grüner Federn. **4** Wenn sie einen sehr hohen Rang innehatten, so trugen sie Halsbänder aus großen, blutroten Perlen und Knochensplittern, die krallenförmig geschnitzt wurden. **5** Greifbare Zeichen königlicher Gunst bzw. eine Auszeichnung für Tapferkeit vor dem Feind waren ein Messing-Armband, *ingxotha*, das nur am rechten Handgelenk getragen wurde, sowie **6** ein Halsband aus ineinander verhakten Perlen, das *iziqu* genannt wurde.

D1 Die Kriegsschilder wurden aus den Häuten sorgfältig ausgesuchter Rinder gemacht; **2** Zur Verstärkung wurden Hautstreifen durch parallel verlaufende Schlitze in der Mitte geflochten; **3** Dann wurde auf der Rückseite ein Stock durch die Streifen gesteckt. **4** Die Spitze des Stocks hatte eine Kerbe, in der als Verzierung ein Stück Fell angebracht wurde. **5** Der Schild wurde entweder am Stock gehalten, an einem Griff aus Tierhautstreifen, oder an beidem. **6a-b** Länge der Schilder; **7** Identifizierung der Schilder - obere Reihe: **(a)** König Shakas Kriegsschild, **(b)** Kriegsschild von uThulwana *ibutho* und **(c)** uDloko *ibutho*, 1879. Mittlere Reihe: **(d)** uMxapho *ibutho* (mutmaßlich) und **(e & f)** zwei Muster von uKhandempemvu *ibutho*, 1879. Untere Reihe: **(g)** uMbonambi *ibutho*, **(h)** uNokhenke *ibutho*, **(i)** iNgobamakhosi *ibutho*, alle aus dem Jahr 1879.

E Junge Krieger in ihrer Kadettenzeit bei einem *ikhanda* Übungsstockkampf. Einer der *izinduna* des Königs, rechts, schaut ihnen zu sowie zwei ältere Jugendliche, links, die der Altersgruppe unmittelbar darüber angehören und bereits einem *ibutho* zugeordnet wurden.

F Eine Zulu-Armee auf dem Vormarsch. Die Armee marschierte in zwei parallelen Regiments-Kolonnen an die Front, wobei an den Flanken *izindibi*-Jungen Matten trugen oder Rinder zum Schlachten vor sich hertrieben. Einzelne Späher spionierten viele Kilometer vor der Armee die Bewegungen des Feindes aus, wobei zwischen ihnen und dem Großteil der Männer eine dichtere Männerwand war, die als Vorhut diente. Hier kehrt einer der Späher zurück und erstattet einem dienstälteren *induna* Bericht. Als Zeichen des Respekts erhebt er seinen Arm und kauert sich nieder.

G Bei Erreichen der Stellung des Feindes stellten die Zulus die versammelte Armee gewöhnlich in einem Kreis auf, dem *umkhumbi*, worauf der dienstälteste *izinduna* eine letzte Ansprache hielt und Anweisungen erteilte. Die *izinyanga*, Ärzte, die auf Arzneimittel spezialisiert waren, die die Männer im Krieg beschützen sollten, schritten die Krieger ab und beträufelten sie mit *intelezi*-Medizin.

H Die beliebteste Angriffsformation der Zulus, die sogenannten "Tierhörner", bei einem Laufkampf mit den Buren 1838 in Aktion. Der "Rumpf", der für gewöhnlich aus erfahrenen Kriegern bestand, schritt rasch auf die Front des Feindes zu, während die Flanken - bzw. die "Hörner" -, die normalerweise aus jungen, ledigen *amabutho* bestanden, auf beiden Seiten ausschwärmten und versuchten, den Feind zu umzingeln.

I Der Schock der Schlacht. Das Gefecht an sich war kurz, jedoch heftig und brutal, ein hautnaher, blutiger Kampf mit Stichwaffen, die schreckliche Wunden schlugen. Unter diesen Bedingungen wurde der kombinierte Einsatz des Schildes und des Stichspeeres perfektioniert.

J Selbst ein siegreicher Kampf hatte normalerweise eine große Zahl verwundeter Zulus zur Folge, und es gab kaum unmittelbare ärztliche Hilfe. Die offenen Wunden wurden mit Gras verbunden, und die Schwerverletzten wurden von Freunden und Verwandten vom Feld geführt. Die Toten wurden in Schluchten, Höhlen von Ameisenbären oder nahegelegenen Getreidemulden provisorisch beerdigt, oder man bedeckte sie einfach mit einem Schild. Das Schicksal der Toten der feindlichen Seite war stets grausig.

K Nach einer erfolgreichen Schlacht, wie etwa Isandlwana, mußten sich diejenigen, deren Geist durch die Berührung mit geflossenem Blut verseucht worden war - also diejenigen, die einen Feind getötet hatten oder selbst verwundet worden waren -

le faire mais, dans tous les cas, on n'appelait les régiments mariés que pour la cérémonie umKhosi annuelle ou en cas d'urgence nationale. Comme l'armée Zoulou n'était rien de plus que les forces combinées des hommes Zoulou en armes, une telle retraite modifiait peu leur style de vie et un guerrier affrontait ses dernières années sans crainte en sachant que son service passé et son grand âge lui valaient le respect de sa famille immédiate mais également de ses contemporains et des plus jeunes.

einem aufwendigen Reinigungsritual unterziehen, bevor sie wieder in die zivile Gesellschaft eingegliedert werden konnten.

L Fortgeschrittenes Alter brachte den allmählichen Rückzug vom aktiven Dienst für den König mit sich. Einzelne traten weiterhin bei ihrem *ibutho* an, so lange ihre Gesundheit es erlaubte, doch wurden die Regimenter verheirateter Männer lediglich für die jährliche umKhosi-Zeremonie oder im Falle des nationalen Notstands herangezogen. Da die Armee der Zulus nichts anderes war als die vereinte Kraft der Zulu-Männer mit Waffen, brachte dieser Rückzug keinen besonderen Wandel für die Lebensart mit sich, und ein Krieger konnte seinem Lebensabend beruhigt entgegensehen, da er sich mit seinem geleisteten Dienst und dem fortgeschrittenen Alter Respekt verdient hatte, der ihm nicht nur von seiner Familie, sondern auch von seinen Gleichaltrigen und den Jüngeren entgegengebracht wurde.